T0066990

LENA OBERDORF

NATIONAL
GEOGRAPHIC
KiDS

ESPN

IT'S A
NUMBERS
GAME!
SOCCER

The math behind the perfect goal,
the game-winning save,
and so much more!

James Buckley, Jr.

Foreword by USWNT Superstar Alex Morgan

NATIONAL GEOGRAPHIC
WASHINGTON, D.C.

TABLE OF CONTENTS

Foreword. 6

Chapter 1: Kickoff! 8

Chapter 2: Line 'Em Up 24

Chapter 3: They Like to Move It, Move It 42

Chapter 4: Goalies Need Math! 62

Chapter 5: Soccer Stats 76

Chapter 6: Trophy Time! 94

Chapter 7: 11 Crazy Numbers 110

Glossary 124

Credits 125

Index 126

International stats are complete at least through the end of 2019.
League and Cup results include the end of the 2019 league seasons.

I'll never forget the first international goal I ever scored. It was October 2010, in Philadelphia. I was 21, and I'd just started playing with the U.S. women's national team a few months before. We were down 1-0 to China when I entered the game as a late sub. Minutes later, Heather Mitts kicked the ball high into the air on the right side of the field. Abby Wambach, my partner in crime up front, chased it down and headed it to me. The goal was in front of me, but two Chinese defenders were closing in. I knew I needed a better angle for my shot, so I used my left shoulder, to knock the defender closest to me off balance. It all happened so fast, but I remember everything about it. I struck the ball hard with my left foot, and boom, 1-1.

Whether we realize it or not, soccer players use math all the time. We talk about angles so much in practice it becomes automatic in games. We don't even think about it. Every time I get the ball within the 18-yard box, I use math to decide if I'm going to shoot immediately, take a touch to prep the shot, or control the ball first. Within seconds. That decision depends on lots of different factors, like where I am, where the goalie is, how fast the ball is going, how fast I'm going (I can get up to 20 miles an hour [32 km/h]!), how level the grass is, what the angle is, and which foot I'm going to use (my left is better than my right!).

Whether you're a math whiz or soccer superstar (or both!), you're bound to pick up some helpful tips in *It's a Numbers Game! Soccer*. This book will explain all the data, digits, and calculations you'll need to get a better understanding of the game—and improve your play on the pitch. Read about some of the greatest stars in the sport and the amazing records they've achieved. Like Kristine Lilly, one of my heroes growing up, who played an unbelievable 354 games for the U.S. women's national team. No one else, man or woman, has competed that many times internationally. I got to play with her in the last six months of her career—before she passed her iconic #13 jersey to me.

No matter if you're new to soccer or practically pro, follow teams around the world or can't resist crunching numbers, this book is for you. Game on!

Alex Morgan

ALEX MORGAN OF THE ORLANDO PRIDE TAKES A SHOT ON GOAL DURING A 2017 MATCH AGAINST THE PORTLAND THORNS.

CHAPTER ONE

KICK

OFF!

Soccer is known as "the beautiful game." Soccer fields are often filled with lush green grass. Bright flags flutter at the corners. The players' uniforms, which pop with color, add to the scene. So does the soccer ball as it flies around the field like a rocket.

However, the game's true beauty is the movement of the players on the grass. Using everything but their hands and arms, they get the ball to do amazing things. And they do so while running at high speeds, leaping great heights, and producing highlight-reel plays at every game.

Let's kick off our trip through soccer numbers by looking at the basics of the game. Lace up your boots, get your kit, and let's hit the pitch! (Don't worry, that will all make sense by the time you finish the book.)

DIGIT-YOU-KNOW?

How many people can pack into soccer's biggest stadiums?

STADIUM, LOCATION	CAPACITY*
Rungrado May Day Stadium, Pyongyang, North Korea	114,000
Camp Nou, Barcelona, Spain	99,354
FNB Soccer City Stadium, Johannesburg, South Africa	94,736
Rose Bowl, Pasadena, California	92,542
Wembley Stadium, London, England	90,310

*In this case, "capacity" means the maximum number of individuals able to sit in a building.

HERE'S *THE PITCH!*

Most people say "the pitch" when talking about the field where a soccer game is played. The term comes from the name for the playing field of an older English sport, cricket.

Each field's exact measurements can differ based on how much room is available in the building or area where the field is placed. However, the Fédération Internationale de Football Association (FIFA), which governs soccer worldwide, sets some basic rules for field size.

For international games, FIFA requires fields to be 110 to 120 yards (100 to 110 m) long and 70 to 80 yards (64 to 73 m) wide. For other pro competitions, FIFA says the field must be 100 to 130 yards (90 to 120 m) long and 50 to 100 yards (45 to 90 m) wide. In the United States and Canada, some Major League Soccer pitches are smaller than international pitches and differ in size because they are in football stadiums. High school and college pitches can be smaller for the same reason. Younger players play on smaller pitches too, with a big field often divided into different sections so multiple matches can take place at once. But no matter the size, all the fields have markings like the ones shown here.

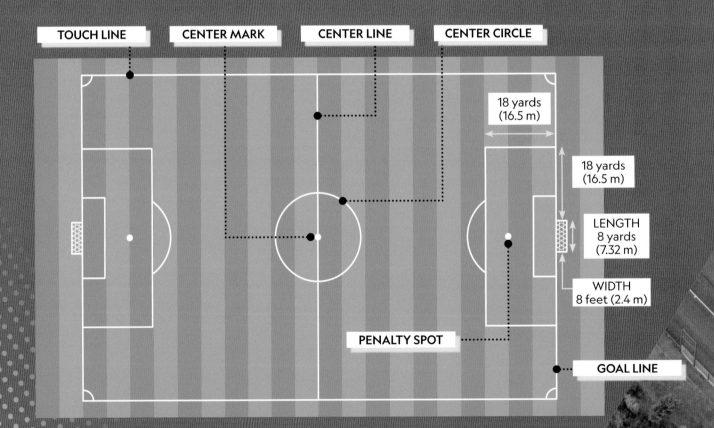

TOUCH LINE   CENTER MARK   CENTER LINE   CENTER CIRCLE

18 yards (16.5 m)

18 yards (16.5 m)

LENGTH 8 yards (7.32 m)

WIDTH 8 feet (2.4 m)

PENALTY SPOT

GOAL LINE

Most of the world calls this sport football. Not the United States! By the time soccer became popular in the U.S., American football was already a big deal. To avoid confusion, the new kick-only sport was named "soccer" after "association football," a term used for the sport in England.

STAT STORY

Want to play soccer inside? No problem! Futsal is a kind of indoor soccer. It is played on gym floors around the world. Invented in Uruguay in 1930, the game features only five players on each side. The athletes use a smaller ball and maneuver around a much smaller area of play. Futsal is a fast-paced game that calls for quickness and great skill.

STATSTARS

Soccer is played on the beach, too. Teams of three to five players, including a goalie, take part in tournaments on the sand. The games are much shorter, since running in sand is pretty tough. Portugal is the 2019 world champion in men's beach soccer. England won the women's title in the 2017 European championship.

PENALTY AREA *CLOSE-UP*

Asoccer field is divided across the middle to create two large boxes, each with a goal at its far end. In front of the goal is a rectangular penalty area. Lines on the field define this important region. The box extends 18 yards (16.5 m) in front of the goal line and 18 yards (16.5 m) to the side of each goalpost. The penalty area is important for several reasons:

- A goalie can use her hands only inside this area. Once she is outside the area, she's considered a regular player and is just allowed to use her feet, body, and head.
- If the defense commits a major foul inside the penalty area, the referee awards the attacking team a penalty kick (PK). This kick is taken against just a goalie from 12 yards (11 m) out. Most often these result in goals. At the 2018 World Cup, for example, PKs scored about 76 percent of the time.
- Offensive players use the white lines to help them know at what angle to take shots at the goal. The lines are a sort of guide for expert players.

A 1902 MATCH IN ENGLAND

A Box Inside a Box

Inside the penalty area is another box that's 6 yards (5.5 m) wide and 20 yards (18 m) long. This is called the goal box. Its main purpose is to show the spot where goal kicks are taken. Goal kicks are kicks made by the attacking team that knock the ball over the end line and out of bounds (but not into the goal, of course!). However, good goalies use this box like shooters use the penalty box—as a guide for where to stand and move. Goalies move with their backs to the goal to block shooters. That makes the goal harder to monitor. How can a goalie keep track of it? He uses the lines of the goal box at his feet.

HISTORY BY THE NUMBERS

Why is the penalty area measured in yards and not meters? By the start of the 20th century, soccer had spread to many parts of the world. And the size of nearly all the field markings had been officially set in meters, the unit used by most countries. But in 1902, the penalty area was introduced in England. At the time, England used yards instead of meters, so the area was set in yards—and it stayed that way.

PENCIL POWER

How many yards wide is the penalty area? Look at the diagram on page 10. Add the length of the goal to the length of each edge on the sides of the penalty area. What did you come up with?

ANSWER: 18 yards on one side, plus 18 yards on the other, plus 8 yards across the goal = 44 yards wide.

THE *GOAL*

The target for anyone shooting the ball is the goal. One goal stands at each end of the field, of course. The soccer goal is supposed to measure 8 by 8, but if you look at a goal, it's not a square! How does that work? Well, the goal must be 8 *yards* (7.32 m) long and 8 *feet* (2.4 m) tall.

Now that you know the dimensions of the goal, can you figure out how many soccer balls would fit into the opening? Math it up! By dividing both the height and the length of the goal by the diameter of a ball and multiplying the result, you'll see the answer is (about) 350. Watch how it's done (all measurements are in inches):

96 (height of goalpost)
÷ **8.9** (diameter of ball)
10.8 balls per side (height)

288 (length of goal)
÷ **8.9** (diameter of ball)
32.4 balls across (width)

10.8 balls
✕ **32.4** balls
349.9 balls

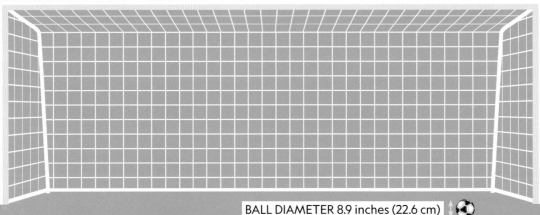

LENGTH
8 yards (7.32 m) OR 288 inches (731.52 cm)

HEIGHT
8 feet (2.4 m)
OR
96 inches
(243.84 cm)

BALL DIAMETER 8.9 inches (22.6 cm)

PENCIL POWER

What is the area of the whole front of the goal? Time to do some math. The area of a rectangle is found by multiplying the shape's width and length. For instance, if a shape is 4 feet (1.2 m) across and 6 feet (1.8 m) tall, the area inside is 24 square feet (2.16 sq m).

So that's the math, but you have to use the right units of measurement, too. It doesn't work to multiply two different units like feet and yards—they have to be the same. So first, you convert 8 yards to feet. (Hint: There are 3 feet in 1 yard.) Then multiply that number by 8 feet and bingo, that's the area of the goal. Try this out for yourself and see if you get the correct measurement!

ANSWER: Each yard in 8 yards equals 3 feet; 8 × 3 = 24 (total number of feet in 8 yards). Area calculation: 24 feet x 8 feet = 192 square feet.

DIGIT-YOU-KNOW?

When is a goal a goal? When 100 percent of the ball has crossed over 100 percent of the goal line. If only a tiny sliver of ball is past the goal line when the goalie stops it, that's not a goal. So play the percentages and just blast it into the back of the net!

THE **BALL**

You can't play the game without the ball! Since soccer kicked off in the 19th century, equipment makers have tried different materials and forms to find just the right ball. Here's how the soccer ball has bounced through the years.

HEAVY LEATHER: The first soccer balls in the 1800s had rubber bladders inflated with air and covered in leather panels. The leather was hand-stitched together. Sometimes the stitches were on the outside. The balls got heavy when used in the rain, since water could seep in.

BETTER LEATHER: By the 1950s and 1960s, the ball was made of 18 separate leather panels stitched around a bladder. The stitching was on the inside. The leather itself was lighter and thinner and didn't hold water as much.

GET IN SHAPE: In the 1960s, a new design really changed the ball. Designers merged 20 hexagons and 12 pentagons to form the sphere. The five-sided shapes were black, and the six-sided ones were white. Many balls still look like this today. Still, scientists wanted an even better ball with a more consistent flight path.

HEAT 'EM UP: Starting in the mid-2000s, developers began using computers to design soccer balls, which allowed them to produce the panels in any shape. And instead of sewing the panels together, they used heat and heavy iron presses to meld the pieces onto the inner ball.

BALL *CHART*

To read this chart on the different sizes of soccer balls, you first need to know a geometry word: circumference. That's the distance around a sphere. Why use different-sized soccer balls? Ball sizes differ by age group, with younger (and smaller) players using smaller soccer balls. Smaller balls are less difficult to control, which makes learning how to play easier.

SIZE	AGES*	CIRCUMFERENCE
5	13 and older	27 to 28 inches (68.5 to 71 cm)
4	12 and under	25 to 26 inches (63.5 to 66 cm)
3	8 and under	23 to 24 inches (58.5 to 61 cm)
Futsal	Any	25 to 26 inches (63.5 to 66 cm)
Beach	Any	26.8 to 27.6 inches (68 to 70 cm)

*These age ranges can vary from place to place. This chart is for AYSO (American Youth Soccer Organization) play. Of course, there's no law against anyone of any age playing with a size 5 ball!

DIGIT-YOU-KNOW?

A hand-stitched ball can take more than three hours to make. Heat-pressed balls come together faster.

HEAT-PRESSED BALL

HAND-STITCHED BALL

SOCCER'S *WEIRD CLOCK*

Five, four, three, two, one ... zero! Game over! Not in soccer, though. While sports like basketball and hockey use a clock that counts down to 0:00, soccer goes the other way around. At the start of the game, the clock is set at 0:00, and it counts up a second at a time. The game's second half starts at 45:00.

There's another wrinkle. While fans and players of those other sports watch the clock like hawks, only one person in soccer really knows when the game will end. That's a type of referee who's known as the fourth official (see page 31). The clock never stops during a soccer game (there aren't even time-outs), but this official is allowed to add "extra time." When a player is injured or there is a long goal celebration or substituted players take a long time walking off the field (they do this on purpose to kill time when their team is ahead), the official adds seconds to his or her clock. At the end of each half, the official lets the fans and teams know how much extra time will be added.

TheFA.com

REFEREE NATALIE WALKER HOLDS UP THE CLOCK SHOWING TWO MINUTES OF ADDED TIME.

A SCOREBOARD SHOWS A TIED MATCH BETWEEN FC PORTO AND MANCHESTER UNITED.

WHO'S IN FIRST?

Teams can't tie in sports like baseball or professional ice hockey. But regular-season soccer games can end in ties. So how do you know which soccer team is on top? When calculating the standings in a league, teams get three points for a win and one point for a tie, known as a draw in soccer. No points are awarded for a loss. At the end of the season, the team with the most points, not the most games won, is number one.

In playoffs, of course, you can't have ties. (Though there can be ties in the early rounds of the World Cup and other tournaments.) In a game where there has to be a winner, teams play overtime. At the top pro level, that means 30 minutes broken into 15-minute halves. If no team scores in that time, they go to a penalty-kick shootout. Each team gets to take five PKs. If they each make the same number of those five, then they keep taking turns until one misses and one scores.

PENCIL POWER

See how these teams finished in their league. Add up the points they should get for each win and each draw and discover who had the most points!

Major League Soccer (MLS) Standings
(Not in order of finish ... that's up to you to figure out!)

TEAM	W	L	D*
D.C. United	14	11	9
Atlanta United	21	7	6
New York Red Bulls	22	7	5
Columbus Crew	15	14	5
New York City FC	16	10	8

www.mlssoccer.com/stats

ANSWERS FROM TOP TO BOTTOM: 51, 69, 71, 50, 56

*D stands for "draw," the soccer word for a tie!

17 LAWS

Soccer is famous among major sports for having the fewest rules, or "laws" as the sport calls them. The NFL and NBA rule books are hundreds of pages long. Major League Baseball needs four umpires on the field to keep all its rules straight. Soccer started with just 14 rules and has added only three more since. Here's a quick look, from 1 to 17.*

1 The field must be green and rectangular with lines to show the penalty area and center circle.

2 The ball must be approved by a league for play and, at the top level, be 27 to 28 inches (68 to 70 cm) around. It should weigh 14 to 16 ounces (397 to 453 g).

3 Each team can have 11 players on the field. One must be a goalkeeper.

4 Players have to wear matching jerseys, shorts, and socks. Goalies can wear long pants. No dangerous jewelry!

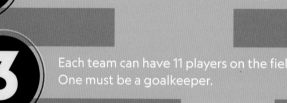

5 The referee is in charge, enforces the laws, and keeps the time.

6 There can be three assistant referees.

7 A standard game is 90 minutes long with two 45-minute halves. The referee can add extra time.

8 Each half starts with a kickoff. A kickoff restarts play after each goal.

9 The ball is out of play when the entire ball goes over an entire line on the side or at the end of the field.

10 A goal is scored only when the whole ball goes over the whole goal line. The team with the most goals wins!

11 When the ball is passed forward, an offensive player must have two defenders between her and the goal.

12 Fouls include kicking, tripping, tackling, holding, or spitting on an opponent. Touching the ball with an arm or hand is also a foul.

13 After a foul, the opposing team gets a free kick.

14 If a foul is committed inside the penalty area, the team that is fouled gets a penalty kick. This is taken from a spot 12 yards (11 m) from in front of the goal.

15 When the ball goes out on the sides, it is put back in by a throw-in taken from over the head. Both feet of the player who's throwing must remain on the ground.

16 When an attacking team sends the ball out over the goal line, the defense takes a goal kick to put it back in play.

17 When a defending team sends the ball over the goal line, the attacking team puts the ball back in play with a corner kick.

*All these rules are for the full 11-on-11 games. Games on smaller fields with small teams and goals might not use all of these rules.

TRY *THIS!*

Who Is the PK Champ?

The penalty-kick shootout is one of the most dramatic events in soccer. Time is up. The score is tied. Now, players from each team face off against the opposing goalie, one player at a time. The team with the most goals after five PKs wins. The pressure on the kickers is huge. A miss might cost their team a championship! For this activity, you're going to stage your own PK shootout.

REMEMBER! Do this activity where there's plenty of space to set up a goal and kick soccer balls.

1 Break up your group of players into two equal-size teams.

Choose a goalie for each team. (You can take turns playing goalie.)

Players from each team alternate taking a penalty kick about 12 yards (11 m) from the goal. You can measure this distance by taking 12 long steps from the goal line. The goalie cannot move ahead of the goal line before the kick is taken. (He can move from side to side, though.)

22

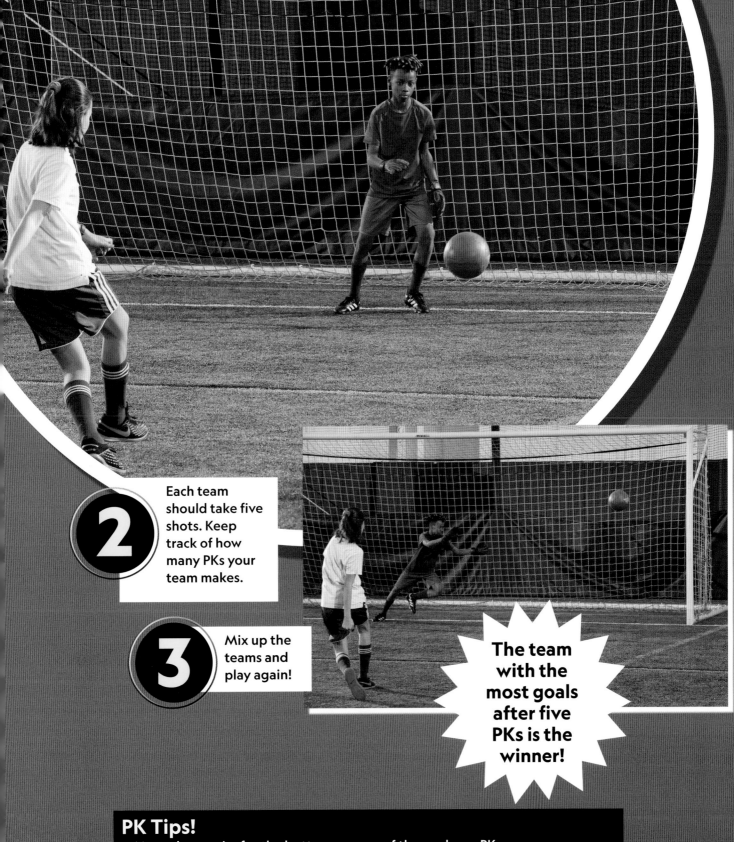

2 Each team should take five shots. Keep track of how many PKs your team makes.

3 Mix up the teams and play again!

The team with the most goals after five PKs is the winner!

PK Tips!

• Most players aim for the bottom corners of the goal on a PK.

• Goalies should be ready to dive to one side or the other. Some goalies take chance dives and hope the player hits the ball to that side!

• Kickers should make sure not to kick the ball too high or it will go over the goal.

CHAPTER TWO

LINE

'EM UP

So we've got a big green pitch and a ball—now we just need players. This chapter takes a look at the people who play the game and the numbers they wear when they play it.

STAT STORY

In 2019, Francis Jacobs became the youngest male player to ever join a professional soccer team in the United States. When he signed on with California's Orange County Soccer Club, Jacobs was 14 years, four months, and 29 days old. That's at least 10 years younger than most of his teammates!

HOW MANY **PLAYERS?**

Soccer has been played with 11 players on each side almost since the sport's beginning. That adds up to 22 players on the field during game time.

Today, younger leagues play with fewer players. This is so that young players can have more chances to touch the ball. The very youngest teams in most youth leagues don't even play with goalies. Why not? The key to learning soccer is not figuring out how to score goals but developing all the skills that you'll need later on. This includes controlling the ball, running on the pitch, and playing defense.

ELEVEN MEMBERS OF THE NIGERIA WOMEN'S NATIONAL SOCCER TEAM POSE FOR A PICTURE IN 2012.

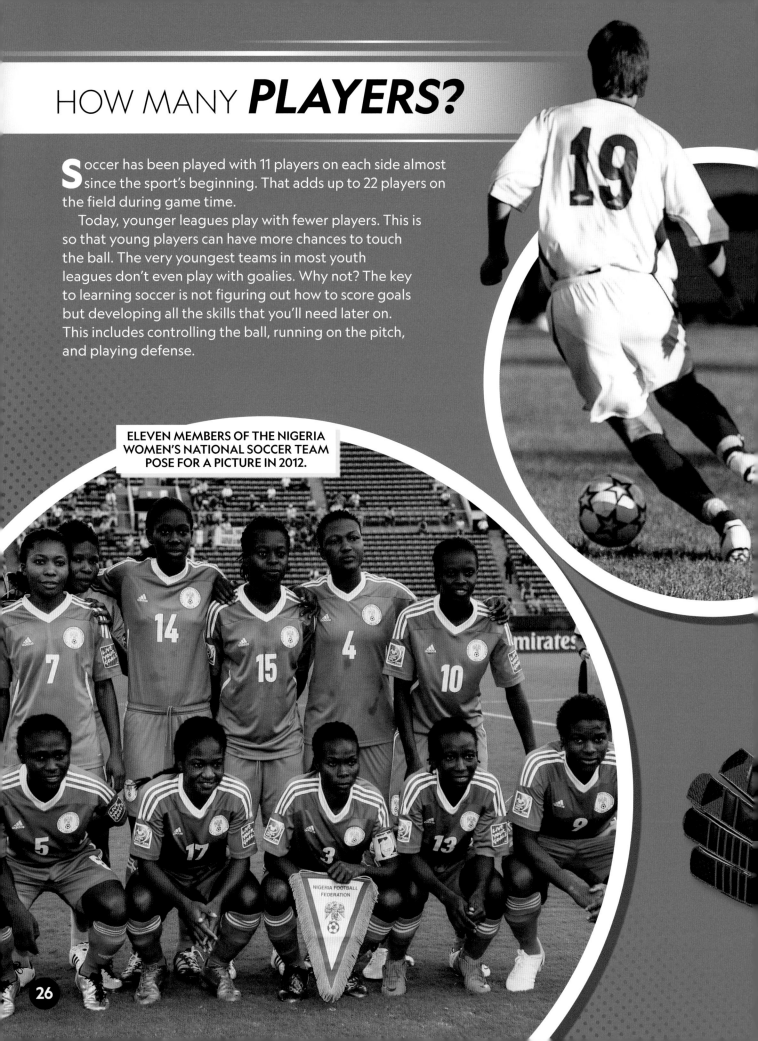

AYSO AGE BREAKDOWN

The American Youth Soccer Organization (AYSO) is the biggest kids' soccer group in the United States. This chart shows how many players AYSO puts on the field in different age divisions.

AGE*	PLAYERS ON THE FIELD	GOALKEEPER?
U5/U6	4	No
U8	4	No
U10	7	Yes
U12	9	Yes
U14+	11	Yes

*"U" stands for "under."

DIGIT-YOU-KNOW?

To find out what percentage of a country plays soccer, you have to divide the number of players by the overall population, and then multiply that number by 100. For example, if two people are soccer players out of a group of 10, then 20 percent of that group plays the game. In one study, FIFA counted heads and did some math to find out which countries had the highest percentage of their population playing in their national soccer associations. The top nations are in the chart below.

Countries With the Highest Percentage of Population in National Soccer Associations

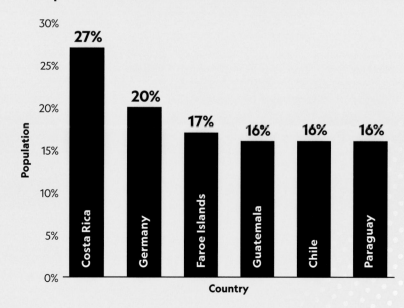

Bar chart — Population (%) by Country:
- Costa Rica: 27%
- Germany: 20%
- Faroe Islands: 17%
- Guatemala: 16%
- Chile: 16%
- Paraguay: 16%

FAB FORMATIONS

Along with the goalie, there are three basic types of soccer positions: defenders, midfielders, and forwards. Defenders play closest to their own goal; midfielders play mostly in the center of the field and are part of both defense and offense; forwards play up front near the opponent's goal. Positions can go by other names that are more specific (center-back, striker, holding midfielder, and so on), but just about every team and formation has players who fill those three roles.

The goalie always stands in the same place—in front of the goal! But how many ways can you arrange a team's other 10 players on the field? The answer is way more than you probably thought! Soccer teams have been tinkering with formations since the game began. The way they name most of the formations is by using number codes. If you know the code, you can see how a team sets itself up. The first number represents the defenders, the second represents the midfielders, and the last number is for the forwards. (The goalie is usually left out of the code since he or she always lines up in the same place.) Check out four of the most popular and familiar soccer formations.

4-5-1

Four central defenders (❷,❹,❺,❸) work together in front of the goal. Two central midfielders (❽,❻) control that important part of the field. Three other midfielders (❼,❿,⓫) often run forward to help the lone forward (❾), or striker. (Strikers are forwards whose main responsibility is scoring.)

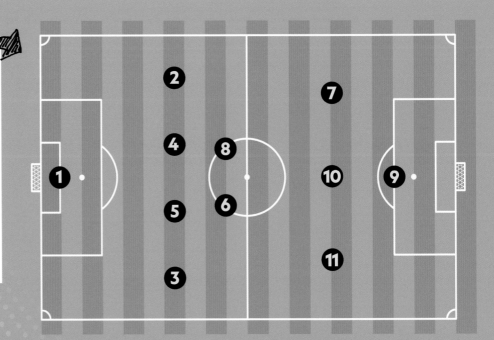

4-3-3

This is a very standard formation used by many youth teams. Four defenders (**2**,**5**,**4**,**3**) form a back line. The center midfielder (**6**) acts as a link between offense and defense, along with outside midfielders (**7**,**8**). The two outside forwards (**11**,**9**), also called wings, try to cross the ball to the center forward (**10**).

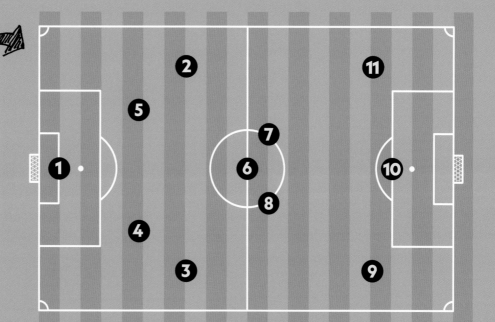

3-5-2

Teams with a very strong center-back on defense use this formation since only three defenders (**3**,**5**,**2**) form the back line. It gives the team a strong midfield of five players (**11**,**6**,**4**,**8**,**7**). The two forwards (also called strikers) (**10**,**9**) play up front near the opponent's goal.

4-4-2

This is one of the oldest formations in soccer. Four defenders (**3**,**5**,**4**, **2**) play at the back. One central midfielder (**6**) focuses on defense, the other (**8**) on offense. The outside midfielders (**11**,**7**) run a lot. They try to score but have to hustle back on defense. Two forwards (**10**, **9**) play close to the opposition's goal.

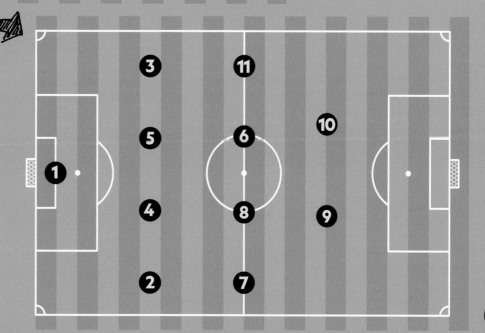

HOW MANY *REFS?*

Along with 22 players, there are at least four more people active on the field in a top-level soccer game. Without them, things would probably get out of hand quickly. They are the game officials—a referee and three assistant referees.

The referee is in charge of the match. She runs on the field with the players and calls fouls. When she sees one, she blows a whistle. The whistle is also used to call for kickoffs and free kicks. The ref's hand signals communicate whether a foul results in a direct kick (where the ball can be shot right into the goal) or an indirect kick (where the ball has to be touched by another player before an attempt at scoring).

Referees can make matches pretty colorful, literally. If a player commits certain fouls—like holding the ball or leaving the field without permission—a ref will hold up a yellow card as a warning. If the player earns a second yellow card for another foul in the same game, the ref will then automatically show a red card. Translation: The player is kicked out of the game and can't be replaced. A ref can skip a yellow card and give a red card right away for a serious foul such as hitting or kicking another player on purpose. This also, of course, means that the player is getting the boot.

Referees have to be in great shape, just like players. They can run as much as 12 miles (19 km) during a game, though they usually don't sprint as hard or as often as the players.

FOUR GAME OFFICIALS EXIT THE FIELD AT HALFTIME DURING A SOCCER MATCH IN FRANCE.

REFEREE GEOMETRY

Yes, refs use geometry! The ref and two of the assistants work in a shape that gives maximum coverage. (See what the third assistant does in the sidebar below!) Each of the two assistants is in charge of one half of the field, but they work on opposite sidelines. The referee then runs generally in a diagonal line that breaks the field into two large triangles (see diagram). Each assistant is in charge of calling offside on their end of the field as well as making the call on which team knocked a ball out of bounds. By creating these triangles, at least two officials are looking at the play at all times.

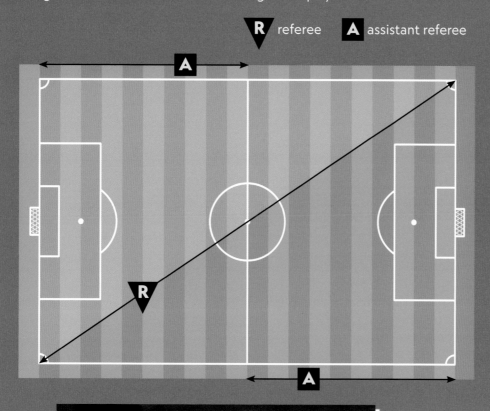

R referee   **A** assistant referee

WAIT, THERE'S ONE MORE!

At nearly all pro and top-level college games, there is one more person to help keep the game running smoothly. Called "the fourth official," he or she doesn't work on the field but next to it at midfield between the two teams. This person announces substitutions and helps the referee announce extra time. The bonus official is also a backup in case one of the other officials gets hurt.

A REFEREE ISSUES A YELLOW CARD CAUTION DURING A 2010 WORLD CUP GAME.

HISTORY BY THE NUMBERS

Why do refs use yellow and red cards? During the 1962 World Cup, many more rough fouls than usual were called. Several players were kicked out. After overseeing that game and another rough game in 1966, an English referee named Ken Aston was inspired by traffic lights. He came up with the yellow-card caution and red-card ejection system. It was first used at the 1970 World Cup and is still used today.

ON THEIR **BACKS**

Unlike American football fields, soccer pitches don't have yard-line numbers painted on them. The only visible numbers on a soccer field are on the players' shirts. What's the story behind these digits?

In soccer's early days, the 11 players who started a game also finished it. There were no subs allowed. So teams just needed 11 uniform numbers ranging from 1 through 11. Also, a popular formation early on was 2-3-5. As you probably guessed, this code stands for two defenders, three midfielders, and five forwards. Officials decided to number players based on this order. That meant that the goalie sported the number 1; the defenders were 2 and 3; midfielders were 4, 5, and 6; and forwards were numbered 7, 8, 9, 10, and 11. So basically, the numbers on the players' jerseys described their positions.

Over the years, what digits 1 through 11 stand for has changed a bit—mostly because there are now more midfielders and defenders than forwards. And there are no official rules when it comes to jersey numbers, so players can wear whatever digit they want. But they love history as much as the rest of us, so you won't see many No. 73s or No. 48s on a soccer pitch. Nope, players tend to stick to the classics—Nos. 1 to 11. In general, you'll most often see these low numbers on the uniforms of national teams and top clubs.

ROBBIE KEANE

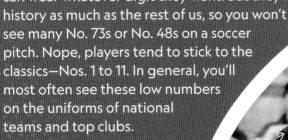

GYASI ZARDES (11) AND JONATHAN MENSAH (4)

GET YOUR KIT!

In England and many other countries, soccer gear is called a "kit." A player's kit includes all the pieces of equipment and attire she needs for a game—shorts, jersey, socks, cleats, shin guards, you name it. So don't forget *your* kit when it's time to play—it's kind of important!

DIGIT-YOU-KNOW?

Top clubs sell tens of thousands of team jerseys a year. Here are the teams with the highest sales from 2018.

TEAM	# JERSEYS SOLD
Manchester United (England)	3,250,000
Real Madrid (Spain)	3,120,000
Bayern Munich (Germany)	2,575,000
FC Barcelona (Spain)	1,925,000
Liverpool (England)	1,670,000
Juventus (Italy)	1,615,000
Chelsea (England)	1,525,000

THE CLASSIC NUMBERS

In soccer today, coaches still use numbers 1 to 11 to describe player positions and the skills and responsibilities that go along with them. But what the numbers stand for differs slightly from the old days of soccer and, unlike in the past, a player's position number might not match up with his or her jersey number. For instance, a player might wear No. 4, but his coach could say, "That guy is my No. 7." Here's a rundown of what coaches today mean when they say that a player is "a classic No. 3" or "the team's go-to No. 11" or "a real No. 8."

1 Still a goalie! They guard the goal mouth and prevent shots from going in.

GARY NEVILLE

2 This is an outside defender, usually on the right side, who works with teammates to keep the other team from scoring.

3 Players sporting this number are outside defenders who focus on the area in front of the goal.

4 These players are central defenders, often on the left side.

5 Though originally used to describe a midfielder, this number has also come to mean a central defender—but one who has attacking (or offensive) skills, as well.

NIKLAS SUELE

6 This is a midfield player who can be on either side or in the center, attacking and defending.

7 They're usually found on the right side in midfield or in the forward line. Teams can often count on No. 7s to race from midfield to the goal line with the ball.

8 This is a central midfielder who keeps things moving by getting the ball to teammates running toward the goal.

9 These players are center forwards, known for scoring and hitting head balls.

MARTA

ARISTOTE MBOMA (FRONT) AND BENCE BATIK (BACK)

10 This number is nearly always given to the team's top scoring threat. The "classic" No. 10 plays near the opponent's goal, scoring often. On some teams, this number is given to the most important player regardless of his or her actual field position. It's a great honor to be a No. 10.

11 Also a forward, this player is often a wing on the left side. And like No. 7, he or she is very good at carrying the ball forward.

DIGIT-YOU-KNOW?

Of course, soccer teams today have more than just 11 members. So official rosters can include many more players. For instance, teams playing in the World Cup have 23 players on their rosters, teams in the National Women's Soccer League have rosters of 18 to 20 players, and the rosters of Major League Soccer teams include 30 players.

CRISTIANO BIRAGHI

WINNING *NUMBERS!*

Who are some of the best players to wear the classic soccer uniform numbers 1 to 11? Check out three cool stats for each of them.

1 GIANLUIGI BUFFON, ITALY

1,000-plus pro games (and counting!)
383 "clean sheets" (aka shutouts)
12 Serie A Goalkeeper of the Year awards

HOPE SOLO, UNITED STATES

202 caps* for U.S. women's team
2 Olympic gold medals
1 Women's World Cup title

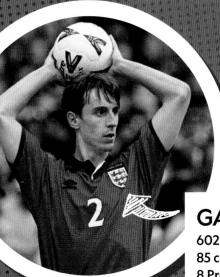

2 CAFU, BRAZIL

142 caps, the most of any player for Brazil
3 World Cup finals, the first player ever to do this
1 Champions League title with AC Milan

GARY NEVILLE, ENGLAND

602 games with Manchester United
85 caps for England
8 Premier League titles

3 ROBERTO CARLOS, BRAZIL

125 caps for Brazil
1 World Cup title
3 Champions League titles

PAOLO MALDINI, ITALY

647 games for AC Milan
8 Champions League finals
1 retired No. 3 (This is a rare honor in soccer, which, unlike many U.S. sports, almost never keeps future players from wearing numbers made famous by stars.)

4 SERGIO RAMOS, SPAIN

600-plus games for Spanish pro soccer teams
161 caps for Spain
1 World Cup title

MICHAEL BRADLEY, UNITED STATES

151 caps for U.S. men's team
16 years old when first drafted for a Major League Soccer (MLS) team
1 MLS Cup with FC Toronto

5 FRANZ BECKENBAUER, GERMANY

390-plus games with Bayern Munich
4 Bundesliga titles and 3 European Cups
1 World Cup title

6 BOBBY MOORE, ENGLAND

667 games in English soccer leagues
108 caps for England
1 World Cup title

BRANDI CHASTAIN, UNITED STATES

192 caps for U.S. women's team
30 goals in international play
2 Women's World Cup titles

7 CRISTIANO RONALDO, PORTUGAL

700-plus career goals (and counting!)
124 goals in Champions League games, an all-time record
5 World Player of the Year trophies

DAVID BECKHAM, ENGLAND**

115 caps for England
6 Premier League championships
2 MLS Cup titles with LA Galaxy

*Any appearance in a national team game earns a player what's called a "cap." The term comes from the early days of soccer, when national players actually got a small cloth cap for each game they played for their country's team.

**Beckham later switched to No. 23 in honor of NBA legend Michael Jordan, who wore the same number.

THE COUNT **CONTINUES**

Keep the numbers coming! Here are more of the best players with the classic uniform numbers. And we'll go above and beyond by including amazing players who wore jersey numbers outside the 1 to 11 range.

8 STEVEN GERRARD, ENGLAND
710 games played for Liverpool
186 goals for Liverpool
114 caps for England

9 ALFREDO DI STÉFANO, ARGENTINA/SPAIN
308 career goals with Real Madrid
8 Spanish league titles with Real Madrid
2 Ballon d'Or awards (given annually to world's top player)

MIA HAMM, UNITED STATES
275 caps for U.S. women's team
158 international goals
2 Women's World Cup titles

10 PELÉ, BRAZIL
1,281 goals (most all-time)
3 World Cup titles
1 designation as a "Brazilian national treasure"

LANDON DONOVAN, UNITED STATES
145 MLS goals (second-most all-time)
58 assists for United States (most all-time)
57 goals for United States (tied for most all-time)

MARTA, BRAZIL
150-plus caps for Brazil
17 Women's World Cup goals (most all-time)
6 World Player of the Year trophies

10 DIEGO MARADONA, ARGENTINA

307 club goals for eight teams, including Boca Juniors and FC Barcelona
34 goals for Argentina
1 World Cup title

LIONEL MESSI, ARGENTINA

622-plus goals for FC Barcelona
91 goals in 2012, an all-time single-year record
6 World Player of the Year trophies

11 DIDIER DROGBA, IVORY COAST

65 goals for Ivory Coast
4 Premier League titles with Chelsea
2 awards for African Player of the Year

13 ALEX MORGAN, UNITED STATES

169 caps (and counting)
107-plus goals for U.S. women's team
2 USA Player of the Year trophies

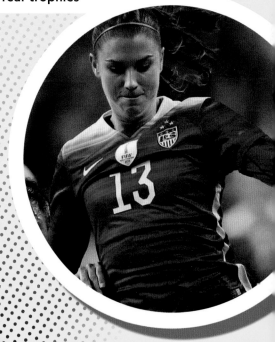

DIGIT-YOU-KNOW?

The great Dutch soccer star Johan Cruyff wore No. 14, an unusually high number for an international hero. Cruyff originally sported a No. 9 jersey. However, during one game in 1970, teammate Gerrie Mühren couldn't find his shirt. Cruyff gave Mühren his No. 9 jersey and grabbed one with No. 14 from a basket of spare shirts. After that, Cruyff insisted on wearing No. 14 whenever possible!

TRY *THIS!*

Fun With Formations

Look back at pages 28–29 for the information about formations. It's time to put on your soccer coach's hat and see if you can come up with some new ones! Cut out 22 small strips of paper—enough to represent the players from two teams. Then, use string to lay out the lines of a mini soccer field like the image at right on a tabletop or on the ground.

Now, arrange 11 paper strips on each side of your "pitch." How many new ways can you come up with to make a formation? Will your teams focus on defense or on attacking? Will you have three main lines of players ... or more?

Materials

- One to two sheets of paper
- String

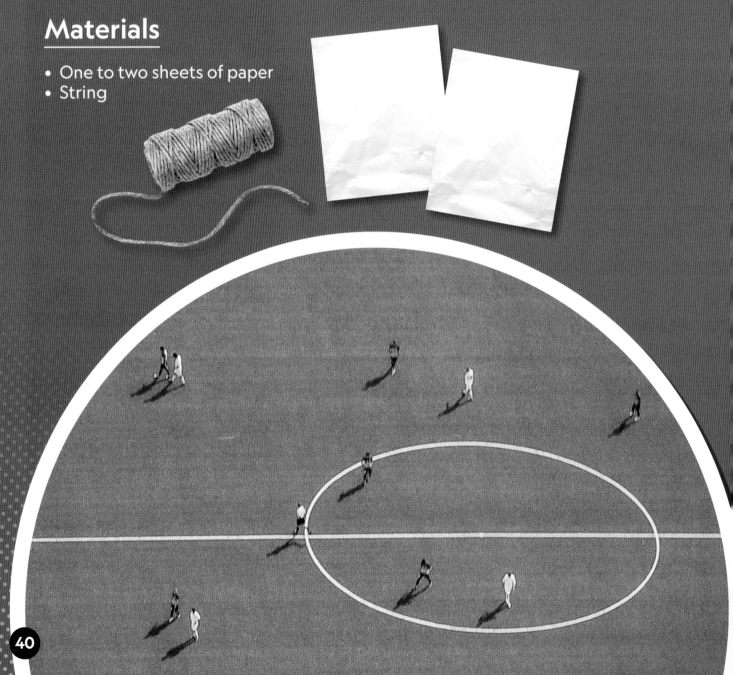

*Pitch lines not to scale

CHAPTER THREE

THEY LIKE TO MOVE IT, MOVE IT

Soccer is a game of constant motion. The ball rolls, bounces, and flies around the field. The players shift positions constantly. The action never stops. All that movement creates a lot of numbers, information, and stats. The ball itself moves the most, so experts have spent a lot of time analyzing how it crisscrosses the pitch. Plus, technology for measuring and tracking players and soccer balls is now playing a big part in the sport. In this chapter, we'll look at all the things that move in the game.

DIGIT-YOU-KNOW?

Soccer players move the ball back and forth across the field, taking shots to score goals. But only shots that are "on target" have a chance at becoming goals. On-target shots are ones directed toward the goal (instead of over or around it). The more accurate those shots are, the better a team will probably do. On average, 26 shots are taken at the goals by both teams during a game, and 9 of those are on target.

OUTSIDE *THE BALL*

Any object hurtling through the air is affected by how the air moves around it. This, of course, includes soccer balls. The way the air flows over the round shape of the ball can alter its speed and flight path. Using different panels on a soccer ball can change how the air rushes around it, which in turn changes how the ball moves. So, how exactly do the panels make a difference? Read on!

NEW TECH

New ballmaking technology in the 2000s allowed companies to create different-shaped panels made of synthetic leather to cover the ball's inner sphere. At first, companies just aimed to create cool designs. Soon though, they realized that the shape of the panels could change how the ball flew. With the right testing, they could make a way better soccer ball.

BLACK AND WHITE

The classic, eye-catching soccer ball pattern of black pentagons and white hexagons (called the Telstar) was created for the 1970 World Cup to make the ball easier to spot on the field by television viewers. Players liked using the Telstar because it was closer to a sphere shape than previous balls. This gave it a more predictable flight path. The ball was popular, but designers thought they could do even better.

14 PANELS

The ball made for the 2006 World Cup was the first one created for this event that left behind the Telstar pattern. The new design had 14 panels of differing sizes. Because there were fewer panels, there were also fewer seams in between the panels, which made the ball smoother than the Telstar. Engineers tested the new design to make sure that the ball would fly true and not spin out of control. Air was shot over the ball in wind tunnels, and experts watched to see whether the air flowed smoothly or not. It did, meaning the ball passed the test!

A WOBBLY PROBLEM

Controversy rolled into the 2010 World Cup when players began using an eight-panel ball called the Jabulani. The ball had been specially made for the games, but players weren't crazy about it. They said that the ball did not curve consistently and that it sometimes "knuckled," or wobbled, as it flew, especially when kicked with very little spin. The reason? The ball was *too* smooth (see the Stat Story on page 45). Its surface caused air to rush over it in a way that disrupted its flight, making it move in unexpected ways.

STAT STORY

Soccer balls look completely smooth, but examine one more closely. The leather on most high-quality balls has a rougher, pebbled surface. It's for the same reason that golf balls have those little dimples. Perfectly smooth spheres actually don't fly very well. The sphere needs something on its surface to "catch" the air as it moves. This creates a straight flight path.

CLASSIC COMEBACK

Making its debut at the 2018 World Cup, the Telstar 18 mixed the best of old and new. It had a pattern similar to the pentagon-hexagon one on the original Telstar. But with only six panels, the ball was more sphere-like than the first version. At the same time, the seams between the panels were rougher and longer than those of the Jabulani to keep the ball from being too smooth. Still, goalies were grumpy about the new ball, which they said continued to wobble a bit in flight.

A LITTLE **KICK**

Soccer players can't pick up the ball and run with it. So how do they get it across the field? Dribbling and passing are the most common moves. Players dribble by giving the ball little kicks over and over again with their feet while running. They can use any part of their feet to do this—each side and the bottom and top. To move the ball to a teammate, they often pass it with the inside of one foot. Check out these must-use moves!

DYNAMO DRIBBLING

Watching a master dribbler is like watching a magician. Sometimes you just can't believe your eyes! Lionel Messi of FC Barcelona is one of the best. The Argentine wonder is able to run at top speed while dribbling around defenders, never losing the ball. Dribbling is a way for players like Messi to control the ball as they move it around the field. And it allows them to gain space from defenders in order to make a successful pass or goal. But players also use dribbling to fool defenders. One move is to roll the ball to the left side of the defender. Then once your opponent steps to the left to intercept the ball, you kick it to the right. Fake-out!

LIONEL MESSI

JORDYN HUITEMA

THE RIGHT SHAPE

Here are the ABC's of passing. First, turn your kicking leg and foot outward so they point to the side. The kicking leg and foot should be positioned so they form a capital L. Lock your ankle and don't bend it. Then move your non-kicking foot so that it forms an L with the kicking foot. The nonkicking foot should be pointing straight ahead at the spot where you want to kick the ball. Keeping your ankle locked, hit the side of the ball with the inside of your kicking foot. Try to make the ball spin forward, not backward. This will make the pass go straighter.

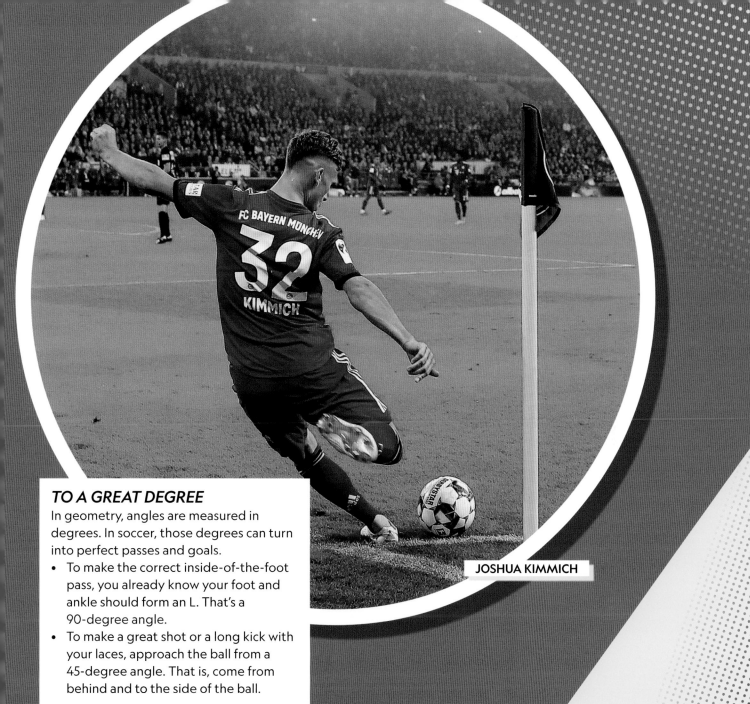

JOSHUA KIMMICH

TO A GREAT DEGREE

In geometry, angles are measured in degrees. In soccer, those degrees can turn into perfect passes and goals.

- To make the correct inside-of-the-foot pass, you already know your foot and ankle should form an L. That's a 90-degree angle.
- To make a great shot or a long kick with your laces, approach the ball from a 45-degree angle. That is, come from behind and to the side of the ball.

STATSTARS

Perhaps the best dribbler in women's soccer is the great Brazilian star Marta. She has won an amazing six Women's World Player of the Year trophies. Not only can she evade defenders with slick moves, but she also is great at making perfect passes to teammates. She's an all-round ball-handling superstar!

BEND *IT!*

One of the coolest things soccer players can do is bend the ball! No, they don't actually twist the sphere into a new shape. Rather, they make it move along a curved path in the air instead of in a straight line. The best players can move a ball several feet off of a straight trajectory. They can curve the ball around a wall of opponents, or they can make the ball fly around a goalie's outstretched hand. Read on to see how it's done.

*Diagram not to scale

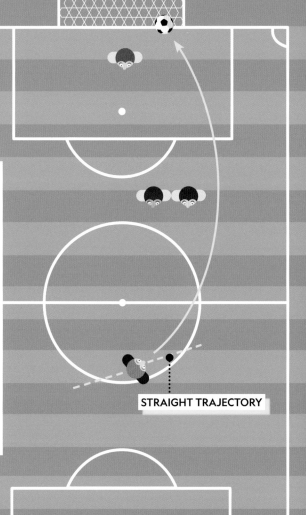

STRAIGHT TRAJECTORY

STARTS WITH A SPIN

Players bend a ball by striking it on one side with the inside of their foot. This causes the ball to spin clockwise or counterclockwise depending on which side of it was hit.

As the spinning ball soars over the pitch, it drags air around it. On one side of the ball, air moves in the same direction that the ball is rotating. On the other side, air moves against the spinning direction. This creates a force that "pushes" the ball in a curved path.

This force is called the Magnus effect, named for German scientist H. G. Magnus, who first described it in 1853.

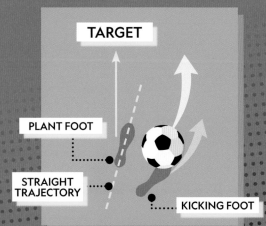

TARGET

PLANT FOOT

STRAIGHT TRAJECTORY

KICKING FOOT

RACHEL YANKEY SHOWS OFF HER BALL-BENDING SKILLS.

STATSTARS

English soccer star David Beckham became famous for his ability to bend a soccer ball. He used this skill to make perfect passes to teammates. He could also swerve a free kick around a wall of players and into the net. Beckham's skills helped him score 65 goals on free kicks, one of the highest totals in soccer history. (Free kicks are awarded by the referee after certain fouls. Opponents must stand at least 12 yards [11 m] away from the ball as the kick is taken.)

TRIANGLE *POWER*

The ball is a sphere. The pitch is a rectangle. So is the goal. There is a circle at midfield and a solid dot at the penalty spot. Those are some of the shapes of soccer. But for players, perhaps the most important shape is a triangle. Watch a soccer game in person from high up in the stands. Over and over, you will see sets of three players on one team spread out in a triangle formation as they work together to move the ball. Each of the players acts as one corner of the moving triangle. Advancing down the field, the sides of the triangle will get longer or shorter or change angles as the players move closer or farther apart from each other. But you watch—the triangle made by the players will still be there.

THE NETHERLANDS' JACKIE GROENEN PASSES THE BALL AROUND AN OPPONENT.

*Diagram not to scale

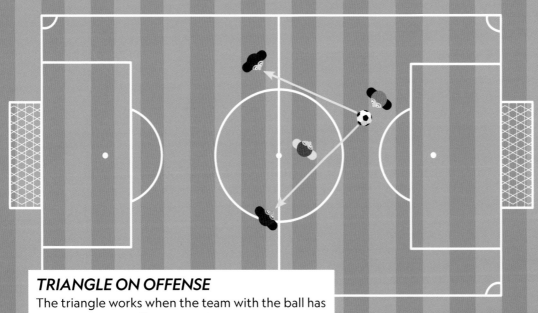

TRIANGLE ON OFFENSE

The triangle works when the team with the ball has three players on offense and the team trying to get the ball has one or two defenders. That means one of the offensive players in the moving triangle is always open. The players in the triangle can keep passing the ball to whomever is open as they move down the field, making it harder for the other team to intercept it.

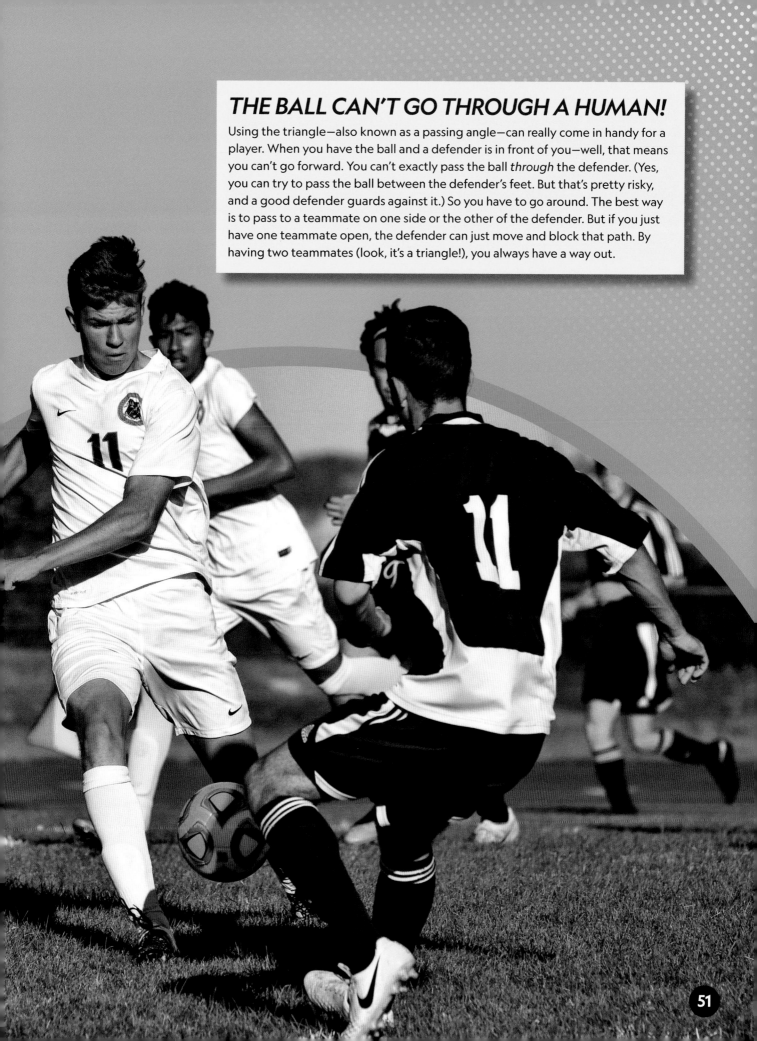

THE BALL CAN'T GO THROUGH A HUMAN!

Using the triangle—also known as a passing angle—can really come in handy for a player. When you have the ball and a defender is in front of you—well, that means you can't go forward. You can't exactly pass the ball *through* the defender. (Yes, you can try to pass the ball between the defender's feet. But that's pretty risky, and a good defender guards against it.) So you have to go around. The best way is to pass to a teammate on one side or the other of the defender. But if you just have one teammate open, the defender can just move and block that path. By having two teammates (look, it's a triangle!), you always have a way out.

TRACKING **MOVEMENT**

Monitors worn on the bodies of soccer players give coaches, trainers, and scientists all sorts of new data to play with. They use the data to show players areas where they can improve. The players strap on small gadgets (usually around their chests) and play a game as usual. The devices measure a variety of things that are going on in the players' bodies as well as what the players are doing on the field. Here are some of the stats that the monitors track.

HEART RATE: Number of heartbeats per minute and how the rate changes as a player moves

DISTANCE RUN: How far, in total, a player moves while on the field

YARDS PER MINUTE: Distance a player runs divided by the number of minutes played. (The stat shows how much ground the player covers during her time on the field.)

SPEED: Fastest speed a player runs at any one point in the game

SPRINTS: How many separate times a player reaches her top or near-top speed in a game

LOCATION: Movement of a player across the pitch (Devices can map out how players travel during the game, creating a sort of grid of everywhere they went.)

THE DEVICES CAN TELL PLAYERS IF THEY NEED TO TAKE A BREAK SO THEY DON'T GET INJURED.

COACHES CAN SEE PLAYERS' STATS IN REAL TIME AS THEY PLAY, THANKS TO HIGH-TECH MONITORS.

PUTTING NUMBERS TO WORK

So. Many. Numbers. How can you keep track of it all? MLS, the premier U.S. soccer league for men, stays up to speed with the Audi Player Index (named after the car company that sponsors it). The index tracks a stack of information—from player movement to passes completed to where a player goes on the field. Points are assigned to or taken away from each MLS player based on his performance on the field. For instance, a midfielder who gets an assist receives 238 index points. A forward who misses a penalty kick loses 354 index points. A defender who wins a tackle is given 52 index points, and so on. All of a player's data is then fed into a computer, which spits out a total number. The higher the number, the more successful and effective the player was. In 2018, for example, the highest Audi Index for the season was 1,266, recorded by Saphir Taider of the Montreal Impact. The score reflected Taider's excellent plays during the season.

SAPHIR TAIDER

WHO RUNS *THE MOST?*

Distance run is one of the most popular and easy-to-understand player tracking stats. Monitors on players' bodies, along with video and computer analysis, can turn all their sweaty steps into numbers. Check out some of these lengthy digits.

LONGEST DISTANCE RUN BY INDIVIDUAL AT 2018 WORLD CUP:
IVAN PERISIC, CROATIA
(7 games)

45 MILES
(72.5 km)

TOP-RUNNING TEAM OF THE SEASON

In the 2018–19 season of the Premier League (England's number one pro league), the top-running team was Arsenal, which averaged more than 70 miles (114 km) of ground coverage per game.

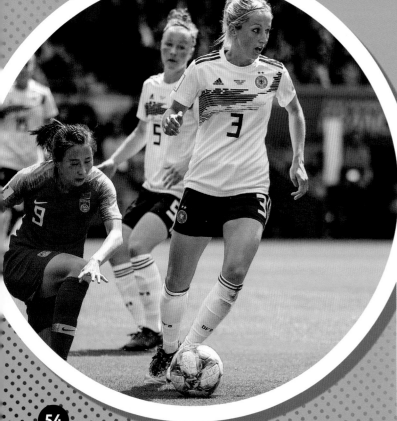

LONGEST DISTANCE RUN BY TEAM AT 2019 WOMEN'S WORLD CUP:
GERMANY NATIONAL TEAM
(5 games)

114.7 MILES
(185 km)

SOCCER VS. THE **SPORTS WORLD**

S ee how soccer compares to other sports in terms of distance run during a game. These are average numbers, not all-time records. Some players in each sport might run more or less in any one game. And cricket matches can last for eight hours, giving them a bit of an advantage in the distance-running department! The other team sports rarely last much more than three hours.

CRICKET: *12.4 MILES* (20 km)

AUSTRALIAN RULES FOOTBALL: *8 MILES* (13 km)

 SOCCER: *6.2 MILES* (10 km)

FIELD HOCKEY: *5.6 MILES* (9 km)

RUGBY: *4.3 MILES* (7 km)

TENNIS: *3 MILES* (5 km)

BASKETBALL: *2.5 MILES* (4 km)

FOOTBALL: *1.25 MILES* (2 km)

BASEBALL: *.0375 MILE* (.06 km)

GOAL CAM TECH

Moving the ball into the goal is the most important part of the game. It can also cause the most trouble. (See page 15 for a refresher on what is and isn't a goal.) Now imagine having to determine whether a goal has been scored when the ball is moving at top speed and a dozen players are in the way of the referee's sight line! Up until around a decade ago, TV broadcast cameras kept catching mistakes made by officials—goals that were not awarded and goals that were mistakenly awarded. Fans saw the mistakes at home, but the refs didn't see them in real time. In 2012, a new technology was tested to solve this problem. The tech utilized cutting-edge cameras that could alert refs when goals were scored.

STAT STORY

Cameras had caught a bunch of referee mistakes before 2010. At the 2010 World Cup, though, two huge mistakes were beamed to audiences worldwide. First, England scored a clear goal against Germany that the referee said did not go in. In another game, Argentina was wrongly awarded a goal against Mexico. TV cameras showed the calls were wrong. Other close calls went the wrong way, and the push to create a tech system sped up.

FRANK LAMPARD OF ENGLAND IS STUNNED AFTER HIS GOAL IS MISTAKENLY NOT COUNTED DURING A 2010 FIFA WORLD CUP GAME.

EYES IN THE SKY

Today, camera technology is an important part of pro soccer. At major tournaments and at soccer stadiums around the world that host top leagues, seven or more cameras are installed and aimed at each goal. That's like having at least 14 additional eyes to help the ref! Each of the cameras is trained on one of the two goal lines. If the entire ball completely crosses either of these lines, a signal is sent to a device on the referee's wrist. It buzzes and beeps to let her know a goal has been scored.

DIGIT-YOU-KNOW?

The cameras grab their images and convert them to a graphic that shows clearly whether the ball went over the goal line or not. The graphic is displayed on a large screen for fans and on the monitor that an official is watching. Within seconds, the official can signal the ref so she can stop the game if a goal was scored ... or wave "play on" if not.

REPLAY FOR REFEREES

Goals are not the only area in which today's soccer referees get help from technology. Refs receive backup from TV camera footage in other cases, too—from possible fouls to the illegal use of hands. With so many cameras now pointing at all the top matches, a new system was created that gives refs a chance to look at instant-replay video when necessary. It's called the video assistant referee (VAR) system. When it comes to making calls in soccer, the biggest problem is time. Soccer does not have time-outs like basketball or football. That means the system has to be super fast so as not to disrupt the flow of the game. Here's how it all goes down.

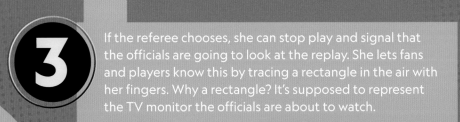

1 Cameras record every moment of every match from many angles.

2 If something happens—a foul, a possible penalty kick, a goal scored after a possible offside call—the VAR system sends a signal to the referee on the field.

3 If the referee chooses, she can stop play and signal that the officials are going to look at the replay. She lets fans and players know this by tracing a rectangle in the air with her fingers. Why a rectangle? It's supposed to represent the TV monitor the officials are about to watch.

4 The ref hustles to a sideline monitor, takes a quick look at the replay, and then makes a final decision. She can award a penalty, take a goal away, or just let the teams play on. The key is that she does this very fast. One study of recent matches that used VAR found that it took the ref an average of about 60 seconds to make each decision.

VAR IN *ACTION*

There are four key events in the game for which referees can use VAR.

GOALS: Along with footage from the 14 cameras aimed only at the goal lines, the ref can see video of any goal from TV cameras set at various angles around the field.

PENALTY KICKS: These are the biggest game-changing moments so refs need to be sure a team deserves to be awarded one. A referee can review any play or contact inside the penalty area to see if a penalty kick should be given.

RED CARDS: When a player gets a red card for a foul, she is ejected from the game and can't be replaced. Refs can check their calls to make sure they are exactly right and reverse their decision if not.

WRONG PLAYER: Sometimes refs give yellow or red cards to the wrong player. VAR can make sure the right player gets "booked."

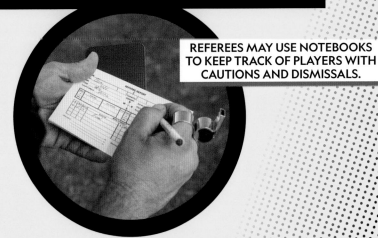

REFEREES MAY USE NOTEBOOKS TO KEEP TRACK OF PLAYERS WITH CAUTIONS AND DISMISSALS.

TRY *THIS!*

Dribble Challenge

In this chapter, you read about how dribblers move the ball. Now, let's see how *you* dribble! You'll need a soccer ball, of course, and some cones. Here are some fun dribbling games you can play.

REMEMBER!
Set up these activities where there's plenty of space in case the ball gets away from you.

Practice Your Speed

Set up a line of five to six cones a few feet apart. See how fast you can dribble the ball weaving back and forth around each cone. Start at one end of the line and return to the same spot. Have a friend time you. What's your best time? To make it interesting, try dribbling with only one foot instead of both!

60

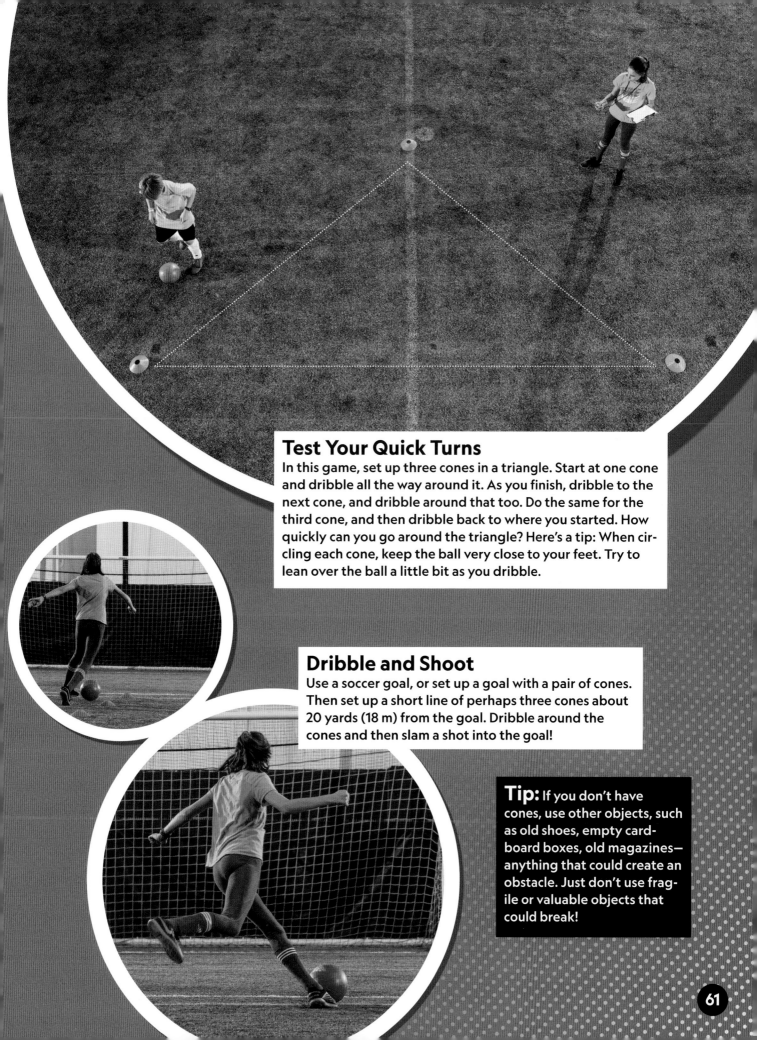

Test Your Quick Turns

In this game, set up three cones in a triangle. Start at one cone and dribble all the way around it. As you finish, dribble to the next cone, and dribble around that too. Do the same for the third cone, and then dribble back to where you started. How quickly can you go around the triangle? Here's a tip: When circling each cone, keep the ball very close to your feet. Try to lean over the ball a little bit as you dribble.

Dribble and Shoot

Use a soccer goal, or set up a goal with a pair of cones. Then set up a short line of perhaps three cones about 20 yards (18 m) from the goal. Dribble around the cones and then slam a shot into the goal!

Tip: If you don't have cones, use other objects, such as old shoes, empty cardboard boxes, old magazines—anything that could create an obstacle. Just don't use fragile or valuable objects that could break!

CHAPTER FOUR

GOALIES NEED

For goalkeepers, the math is easy: A zero is good; anything else is not. OK, maybe it's not *that* simple. Goalies also need to know the dimensions of the penalty area and geometry. This chapter covers the math that gives goalies a major assist.

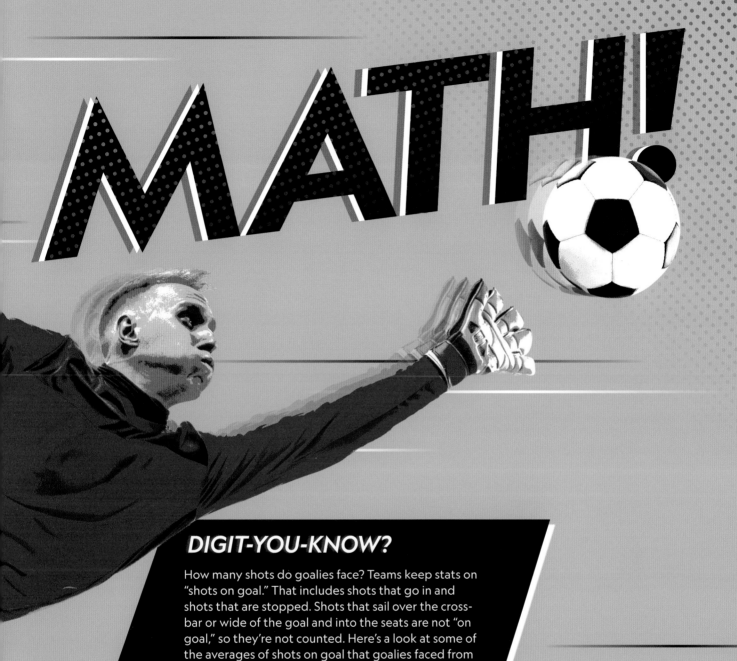

MATH!

DIGIT-YOU-KNOW?

How many shots do goalies face? Teams keep stats on "shots on goal." That includes shots that go in and shots that are stopped. Shots that sail over the cross-bar or wide of the goal and into the seats are not "on goal," so they're not counted. Here's a look at some of the averages of shots on goal that goalies faced from top teams in different leagues in the 2018–19 season.

TEAM, LEAGUE	AVERAGE SHOTS ON GOAL PER GAME
Manchester City, Premier League (England)	19.9
Napoli, Serie A (Italy)	19
Bayern Munich, Bundesliga (Germany)	18.9
Juventus, Serie A (Italy)	17.1
Real Madrid, La Liga (Spain)	16.2

THE GEOMETRY OF **GOALKEEPING**

The most important kind of math for goalkeepers is geometry. A goalie, or keeper, who understands the angles of geometry will be better than one who doesn't. But you can't carry a geometry compass out onto the field, and most games won't stop for you to measure an angle with a protractor. So how do goalies use geometry to win? It's diagram time, soccer fans!

*Diagrams not to scale

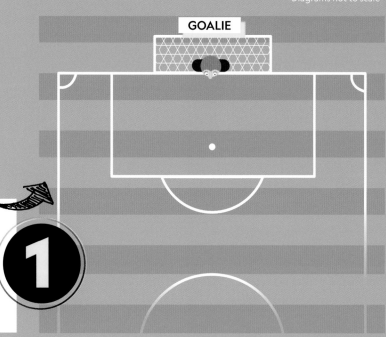

GOALIE

1

DON'T STAY ON THE LINE

It might seem like standing on the goal line is a good place for a goalie. It rarely is. Goalies need to be in front of the line and must move constantly from side to side across the goal. Why not stay on the goal line? Geometry! Keep reading.

2

CUT THE ANGLE

When a player is preparing to shoot, the goalie moves out toward the shooter. By doing this, the goalie cuts the angle. That is, she decreases the angle the player has to successfully kick the ball into the net. So the keeper protects *more* of the goal by moving forward than she could protect standing on the line. In the left-side diagram below, the goalie faces a shot, and clearly the shooter has lots of room. In the diagram on the right, the goalie has moved out several yards from the goal. Suddenly, the spaces the shooter can aim for are very tight.

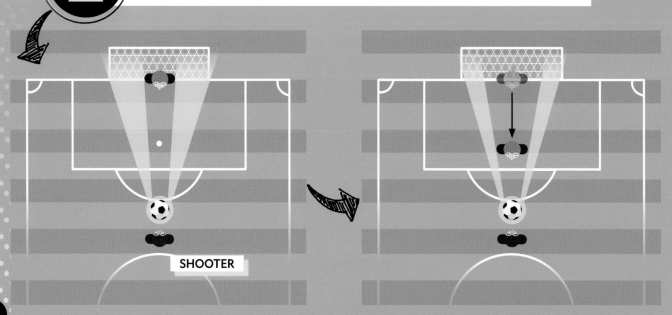

SHOOTER

3 MOVE, MOVE, MOVE

As the ball moves side to side across the field, goalies need to move with it—even if the ball is at the other end of the pitch! Goalies move basically in an arc in front of the goal, traveling to the left when the ball is on the left and to the right when the ball goes right. Good goalies shuffle side to side, they don't cross their feet.

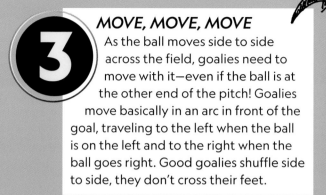

STATSTARS

Manuel Neuer, a top goalie for both the German team Bayern Munich and Germany's national team, has added a new wrinkle to goalkeeping: the sweeper-keeper. "Sweeper" is an old name for a team's last defender in front of the goalie. Remember that once a goalie leaves the penalty area, he can't use his hands. Well, Neuer is so good with the ball on his feet that he plays farther from the goal than many other goalies. His teammates can depend on him to make plays behind them, even without his hands. So, he's basically acting as a keeper *and* a sweeper.

THE NEAR POST

Now that you see how geometry helps goalies, here's a look at the most important piece of equipment on the field for the keeper: the near post. In soccer, the near post is the goalpost that is closest to the side of the field where the ball is coming from. So if the goalie is looking out on the field and the player with the ball is to his right, then the near post is also on the goalie's right. Check out the diagram on this page. The goalie is playing "tight" to the near post. This allows the keeper to block the shortest and easiest shot for the player. That means the shooter has to try to kick or curve the ball around the goalie, which is a harder shot. Making an opponent try a harder shot right away gives the goalie an advantage. Protect the near post!

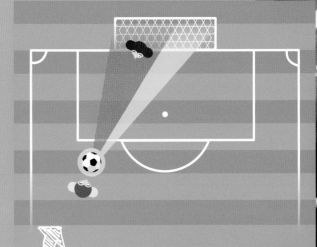

*Diagram not to scale

The goalie stands by the near post, blocking the easiest path for the ball (shown in orange). To get in, the ball would have to move in a path around the goalie (shown in yellow).

STATSTARS

Lev Yashin starred for the pro team Dynamo Moscow for more than 20 years. He also helped the Soviet Union's national team win the 1956 Olympic gold medal. (History lesson: The Soviet Union was a country that formed in 1922 and collapsed in 1991, after which a huge chunk of it became present-day Russia.) Yashin was the first really big goalie superstar. Known as the Black Spider for his black clothes and his long limbs, he set the standard for athletic, diving goalies. In more than 250 of his 800-plus games for club and country, he allowed zero goals!

GOALKEEPER DIEGO ALVES MAKES
A SAVE BY THE NEAR POST.

BUILDING A **WALL**

No, teammates aren't laying brick to construct the outside of a building! In soccer, a wall is a lineup of defensive players who help a goalie stop free kicks. And once again, geometry is the keeper's friend. Remember the way that a goalie cuts the angle? This is what the wall tries to do on a free kick. Teams are allowed to set up a wall 10 yards (9 m) from the spot of the free kick. The referee marks off the distance. The goalie sets up the wall to protect the near post. Then the goalie moves to cover the far post. Now, a great kicker might be able to boot the ball over the human wall; but that should give the goalie time to move over to make a save. Without the wall, many free kicks would probably end up as goals.

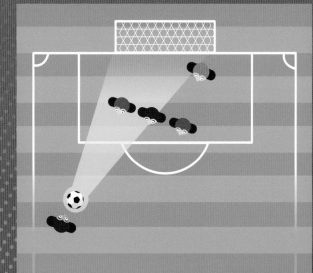

*Diagram not to scale

Keepers arrange the edge of the wall to line up with the near post.

DIGIT-YOU-KNOW?

Walls can include as many players as the goalie wants. However, most walls are only two to three players wide when the kick is on a side of the goal. For kicks more directly in front of the goal, up to five or six players might be lined up.

PLAYERS FROM THE REPUBLIC OF IRELAND WOMEN'S NATIONAL SOCCER TEAM FORM A WALL TO STOP A FREE KICK.

SIX QUICK *SECONDS*

Once the goalie has the ball in her hands, she can throw it to a teammate or kick it (usually by punting it) down the field. She can also put it on the ground and just play it with her feet by passing to a teammate. Well, actually, she could dribble the length of the field and try to score if she really wanted, but that's not very likely to happen! This is important, though: She has only six seconds to make a choice and get the ball out of her hands. Six seconds moves pretty fast, so planning ahead is very important. Here are some pointers goalies keep in mind when deciding how to pass the ball.

GOALIE DROPPING BALL

AIM WIDE
Goalies should almost never throw or kick the ball right to the middle of the field, especially in their half. If the ball goes to an opponent by mistake, that creates an instant threat. On the other hand, throwing it to the side is less risky. When throwing it out, look for a teammate on the wings.

Bonus tip: By running across the penalty area before throwing, the goalie can change the whole direction of her team's attack. For instance, if she picks up the ball on the left and then runs to the right to throw, her team can quickly race to the right side as well. The opponents will have to catch up!

HOPE SOLO

HIGH ARC

Punts are big kicks that the goalie does, dropping the ball from his hands as he swings his kicking foot. These kicks usually send the ball in long, high arcs (called parabolas in science-speak). Either team can try to run to where those kicks will land, so punts are better for clearing the ball out of a team's end than for aiming at a teammate.

BRIAN ROWE

LOOK, NO HANDS!

Sometimes it is better for a goalie to just kick the ball from the ground without picking it up. Good goalies can be more accurate with kicks like this than with punts. Also, if the ball was passed back to them by a teammate, they can't use their hands, only their feet!

TIM HOWARD

DIGIT-YOU-KNOW?

Six seconds was not always the rule. Until 1998, goalies could only take four steps with the ball in their hands. But there was no time limit, so when goalies had the ball, things often slowed down. The new rule was designed to speed things up.

STOPPING *PKs*

FILIP DAEMS (9) SCORES A GOAL BY PENALTY KICK AGAINST GOALKEEPER SVEN ULREICH.

Imagine: There's a collision between players in the penalty box. One player hits the turf, a whistle blows, and the fans roar! The referee points to the penalty spot. The goalie's heart drops—the opposing team has been awarded a penalty kick (PK).

PKs are generally a goalie's least favorite play. It's just him against the kicker, with no defense in front of him. And he can't move forward from his line until the ball is kicked (though he can move side to side).

Penalty kicks can move more than 80 miles an hour (129 km/h). That gives a goalie less than a tenth of a second to react and start moving. Most keepers start a bit early and try to guess which side the kick will go to.

DIGIT-YOU-KNOW?

To dive or not to dive, that is the question. In most leagues, more than 75 percent of penalty kicks end up in the goal. Goalies need to study where those kicks go so they can decide whether to dive for a save or not. The chart below displays info from past international tournaments such as the World Cup and the percentage of kicks that made it into the goal. Shots that went over or around the goal are not included. The red shaded areas are where you have the best chance for a save. The top corners, of course, are the hardest.

GOAL SCORING WHEN ON TARGET

CROSSBAR

100.0%	100.0%	100.0%	100.0%	100.0%
85.7%	81.6%	94.4%	78.9%	80.8%
92.9%	66.7%	88.9%	61.8%	90.6%

GOALPOST

GOALPOST

GROUND

SCIENCE STUFF: TAKING A CHANCE

The chart on page 72 focuses on the percentage of successful PKs during international matches. This chart shows the most effective way that any goalie can move to block one of these shots. A lunging dive from a standing start gives the goalie a chance to stop some PKs. This diagram from the University of Bath in England shows the probability (or chance) of making a save on a kick traveling at 80 miles an hour (129 km/h). Within the diving arc, the chances are 50-50. If the shooter gets outside the arc, the odds of a save go way down.

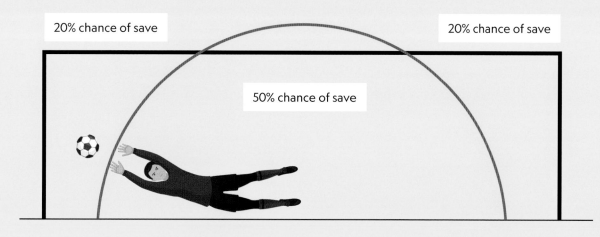

20% chance of save

20% chance of save

50% chance of save

STAT STORY

In 1999, U.S. defender Brandi Chastain got all the headlines for making the penalty kick that won the Women's World Cup during a PK shootout. However, her kick would not have been the winner without her goalie! Earlier in the shootout against China, goalie Briana Scurry dove to her left to make a brilliant save of a kick by player Liu Ying. That opened the door for Chastain's winning kick.

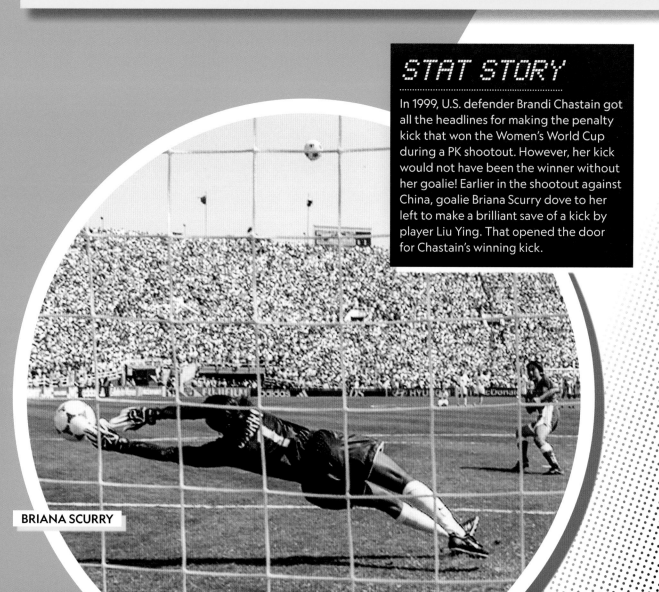

BRIANA SCURRY

TRY *THIS!*

Go Into Goalie Mode

OK, geometry geniuses, let's play goalie! For this activity, you just need a ball (or a few balls), a couple of cones or a soccer goal, and some pals. If you don't have a goal, set up the cones to create one. You can make it the full 8 yards (7.32 m) across or smaller if that's easier. Then take turns playing goalie. The key is to learn how to cut the angle and protect the near post.

REMEMBER!
Do this activity and set up your goal where there's plenty of space.

First, have your friends take shots while you only stand on the goal line. Don't move off it while you try to make saves. Then, start to come off the line to cut the angle. Stay close to the near post, but move toward the person shooting the ball. You'll quickly see how much easier it is to make a save this way. (Don't worry, some shots will get by you … nobody's perfect!) Take turns being the shooter and the goalie. Who can stop the most shots? Keep track and award the winner the Golden Glove!

The Golden Glove is an actual award given at the end of a World Cup competition to the best goalie of the tournament. You probably don't have one of those lying around to give *your* winning goalie, but a high five works well too!

CHAPTER **FIVE**

SOCCER

STATS

Soccer doesn't have nearly as many stats as some other sports. It's a pretty simple game. Score the most goals, and you win. So it makes sense that the goal-scoring numbers are the biggest deal in soccer stats. This chapter breaks down scoring records among league and international competition. It also looks at assists and goalkeeping records.

STAT STORY

When TV broadcasters describe how a goal was made, you might sometimes hear them say that it went "right into the Upper V!" That's a nickname for the upper corners of the goal. Making a perfectly placed shot right under the crossbar and inside the goalpost is tricky, but it's almost guaranteed to be out of reach of the goalie. Then V can be for victory! Another way to describe this shot is "into the Upper 90." That means the 90-degree angle formed by the goalpost and the crossbar.

7 WAYS TO SCORE

So how can a player put the ball in the goal? Let's break down the seven key ways. Three are related to the player's body, three are types of kicks used in certain situations, and the seventh is every player's nightmare.

1 USING THE FOOT:
Well, this is the obvious one. Players use their feet all the time to give the ball standard kicks (read on to find out about other kicks used under certain circumstances). Good players, though, can kick equally well with either foot. They also learn how to use the top and both sides of each foot. Experts can sometimes even kick with their heel.

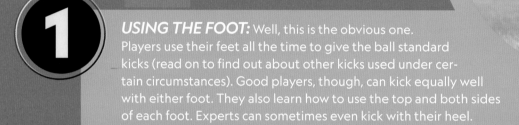

2 USING THE HEAD:
This is for older players only. Young players should wait until they are properly coached to hit the ball with their noggins.

The best way to knock the ball in with the head is by striking it with the forehead. Swing your body toward the ball from the chest, not the neck.

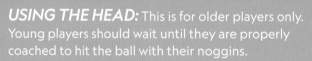

SARA LARSSON

3 USING THE BODY:
As long as the ball doesn't hit your hands or arms, you can knock in a goal with any other part of your body. It can bounce off your chest or your stomach or deflect off your back. Players have scored with their thighs and knees as well.

DIRECT FREE KICK: When the referee awards a direct-kick foul, the team that is kicking can try to smack the ball from the location of the foul right into the goal. This is hard, of course, but free kicks are some of the most exciting goals in the game.

CORNER KICK: This doesn't happen often, but a talented player can use a corner kick to get the ball directly into the goal from one corner of the field by bending, or curving, it.

PENALTY KICK: This is the kick of death, remember? Taken from 12 yards (11 m) against only the goalie, it's usually an easy goal.

OWN GOAL: This is the worst kind of goal. It a defender accidentally knocks the ball into the goal he is guarding, it counts for the opponent's offense. It's always a mistake, not on purpose, but it's embarrassing. Still, it happens to the best players in the world!

TROY DEENEY REACTS TO SCORING AN OWN GOAL DURING A MATCH.

"GOOOOAALLL!"

ABBY WAMBACH

The biggest goals players can score are the ones they score for their country at the Olympics or World Cup. The right goal at the right moment can make these players instant national heroes. Some of the biggest names in soccer history, in fact, are among the Top 10 all-time goal scorers in international competition. But you might find some surprises!

WOMEN

PLAYER	INTERNATIONAL GOALS
1. Christine Sinclair,* Canada	186
2. Abby Wambach, United States	184
3. Mia Hamm, United States	158
4. Kristine Lilly, United States	130
5. Birgit Prinz, Germany	128
6. Carli Lloyd,* United States	122
7. Julie Fleeting, Scotland	116
8. Patrizia Panico, Italy	110
9. Marta,* Brazil; Elisabetta Vignotto, Italy; Alex Morgan,* United States	107
10. Sun Wen, China	106

*Still playing as of 2020

DIGIT-YOU-KNOW?

Stats are recorded on how often goals are scored from corner kicks, free kicks, and penalty kicks. Such plays are called "set pieces." At the 2018 World Cup, 70 "set piece" goals were scored. That was 43 percent of the total goals scored. A record 22 of those were from penalty kicks.

MEN

PLAYER	INTERNATIONAL GOALS
1. Ali Daei, Iran	109
2. Cristiano Ronaldo,* Portugal	99
3. Ferenc Puskas, Hungary	84
4. Kunishige Kamamoto, Japan	80
5. Godfrey Chitalu, Zambia	79
6. Hussein Saeed, Iraq	78
7. Pelé, Brazil	77
8. Sándor Kocsis, Hungary; Bashar Abdullah, Kuwait	75
9. Sunil Chhetri,* India	72
10. Kinnah Phiri, Malawi	71

*Still playing as of 2020

ALI DAEI

STATSTARS

Swedish star Zlatan Ibrahimovic and Portuguese hero Cristiano Ronaldo have played a lot of games. And they've scored a lot of goals. In fact, over the course of their careers, they've both scored at least once in each minute of the 90 minutes that make up a game. (That means that in one game they played, they scored during minute one; in another game, they scored during minute two; and so on, all the way through minute 90.)

CRISTIANO RONALDO

WORLD CUP **WONDERS!**

Scoring goals in the World Cup is the best of the best. If you want to be a top scorer in this tournament, first you and your team have to make it into a lot of World Cups. Only a handful of players have been able to play in more than a couple of these tournaments. Then once you're there, you have to show great scoring abilities. Check out players who accomplished both of these feats, and scored their way into World Cup history.

MIROSLAV KLOSE

MEN'S WORLD CUP SCORING LEADERS

PLAYER	GOALS
Miroslav Klose, Germany	16
Ronaldo, Brazil	15
Gerd Müller, Germany	14
Just Fontaine, France	13
Pelé, Brazil	12
Jürgen Klinsmann, Germany	11
Sándor Kocsis, Hungary	11
Gabriel Batistuta, Argentina	10
Teófilo Cubillas, Peru	10
Grzegorz Lato, Poland	10
Gary Lineker, England	10
Thomas Müller, Germany	10
Helmut Rahn, Germany	10

DIGIT-YOU-KNOW?

Just Fontaine scored all 13 of his goals in 1958. Not surprisingly, that is the record for a single World Cup tournament.

MARTA

STAT STORY

In the final game of the 2015 Women's World Cup, U.S. star Carli Lloyd shocked everyone in the stadium—especially the goalie from Japan—by cracking a high, arcing shot from about 50 yards (45.7 m) from the goal. It was Lloyd's third goal of the game. (When a player scores three goals in one game, it's known as a hat trick.) In fact, it was her third goal in just the first half, part of the four amazing goals the United States scored in 16 minutes to seal their second World Cup triumph.

WOMEN'S WORLD CUP SCORING LEADERS

PLAYER	GOALS
Marta, Brazil	17
Birgit Prinz, Germany	14
Abby Wambach, United States	14
Michelle Akers, United States	12
Sun Wen, China	11
Bettina Wiegmann, Germany	11
Cristiane, Brazil	11
Ann-Kristin Aarones, Norway	10
Heidi Mohr, Germany	10
Christine Sinclair, Canada	10
Linda Medalen, Norway	9
Hege Riise, Norway	9
Alex Morgan, United States	9

LEAGUE *LEADERS*

Who are the top all-time goal scorers in the key leagues around the world?

FIRST DIVISION,* ENGLAND
JIMMY GREAVES
(1957–1977)
357

BUNDESLIGA, GERMANY
GERD MÜLLER
(1964–1982)
564

LA LIGA, SPAIN
LIONEL MESSI
(2004–present)
433**

SERIE A, ITALY
SILVIO PIOLA
(1929–1954)
274

*Existing from 1888 to 1992, the First Division came before England's Premier League.

**Through February 2020

SÉRIE A, BRAZIL
ROBERTO DINAMITE
(1971–1991)

190

MAJOR LEAGUE SOCCER, UNITED STATES
CHRIS WONDOLOWSKI
(2005–present)

159**

NATIONAL WOMEN'S SOCCER LEAGUE, UNITED STATES
SAMANTHA KERR

77**

(2013–present)

DIGIT-YOU-KNOW?

What scores are the most common in soccer games? One report showed the following as the scores most often reported:

SCORE	PERCENT OF GAMES[†]
1–0	16
2–1	14
2–0	12
1–1	12
3–1	8
0–0	7
3–0	6
2–2	5

†These add up to 80 percent of games played. The other 20 percent includes all the other combinations of scores not listed here.

TRACKING **KEEPERS**

Goalies care most about one stat: wins. Of course, the best way to help a team win is to allow no goals. So the most important goal-keeping stat is simply called goals allowed. The lower that number is, the better. But there are other ways to track how well goalies are doing.

SAVES

If a goalkeeper prevents a shot from going into the goal, that's called a save. Keepers don't have to catch the ball for a save; they can push or punch the ball away. Just as long as it doesn't go in. Saves are only awarded for shots that would have gone in, not for catches made on a ball that would have missed the goal.

SAVE STAT:
Tim Howard of the United States set a World Cup record with 16 saves in a 2014 game against Belgium.

SAVE PERCENTAGE

This number is found by dividing the number of saves a goalie has made by the total number of save chances. So if a goalie faces 15 shots in a game and saves 12 of them, you'd divide 12 by 15 to see that her save percentage is 80 per-cent. For most pros, this is a pretty high number. Check out the math:

$$12 \div 15 = 0.8$$
$$0.8 \times 100 = 80\%$$

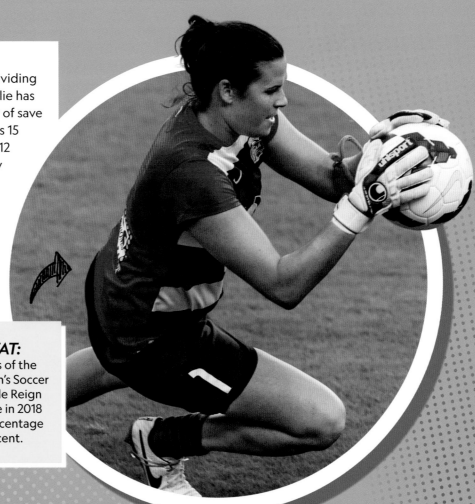

SAVE STAT:
Lydia Williams of the National Women's Soccer League's Seattle Reign led that league in 2018 with a save percentage of 83.6 percent.

PENALTY KICK SAVE PERCENTAGE

Stopping a penalty kick is a huge deal for a goalie. These shots almost always go in. But some keepers have a knack for deflecting them, thrilling their teammates and frustrating opponents. Divide the number of penalty kicks stopped by a keeper by the number taken and you get the keeper's penalty kick save percentage. So if a keeper faces 20 PKs and stops 5, her save percentage is 5 divided by 20. That equals 0.25. Multiply that by 100 to turn this into a percentage, and you get 25 percent.

$$5 \div 20 = 0.25$$
$$0.25 \times 100 = 25\%$$

SAVE STAT:
Diego Alves of Flamengo in the Brazilian Series A league is regarded as one of the top penalty-savers in the game. In 2018, he stopped more than 40 percent of penalties taken against him.

DIGIT-YOU-KNOW?

How long can a goalie go without giving up a goal? They keep track of these things! The world record was set by Mazarópi, who played on the Brazilian team Vasco de Gama. In the 1977–78 season, he kept his net empty for a total of 1,816 minutes. That's more than 20 full games in a row.

CLEAN SHEETS

This is soccer's fancy way of saying a shutout. Goalies who do not allow a single goal in a game have produced a clean sheet.

SAVE STAT:
The all-time record for clean sheets in England's Premier League is 228 by goalie Petr Čech, who began playing in 2004.

HELPING OUT: *ALL ABOUT ASSISTS*

Soccer players can't score alone. One against 11 just wouldn't be fair. Teammates who make a pass that leads directly to a goal can be awarded an assist. There are no points given for assists, but fans and coaches know that players with lots of assists are hugely important to a team. Here, we'll give you an assist in learning more about players who help out with assists.

MR. ASSIST

There aren't worldwide "official" records for most assists in a career, because rules for what counts as an assist vary from league to league. But we do know that the Premier League's all-time Mr. Assist is Ryan Giggs. He racked up 162 assists from 1992 to 2014 playing for Manchester United. He also found time to score 109 goals when he wasn't setting up teammates.

MS. ASSIST

For the U.S. women's team, Mia Hamm gets the top spot on the all-time assists list. She played from 1987 to 2004 and was known mostly for her goal-scoring. However, she created goals for teammates with 144 assists, the most in U.S. women's soccer history.

STAT STORY

The Fédération Internationale de Football Association (FIFA), which runs the World Cup, suggests different possibilities for what counts as an assist, but they're not official. Some leagues give an assist to a player who earns a penalty kick, if someone else actually takes the PK. In some cases, two players can get assists for the same goal if the scorekeeper thinks the second player really was vital.

ASSIST KING?

Gathering all the assist records from leagues around the world and throughout history has not really been done. But check out the numbers for this amazing player: Lionel Messi. He has recorded more than 282 assists for Barcelona and Argentina. And he is adding to that almost every time he steps onto the pitch. Messi's ability to push passes right where teammates can use them is almost spooky. He is able to see perfect places to make passes while everyone else is dazzled by his dribbling.

TWO NEW *STATS*

Soccer is a bit behind other sports in using advanced math (called analytics by sports experts) to measure players and what they do. Two newer soccer stats are trying to make a dent in that.

POSSESSION PERCENTAGE

A great way to make sure that your team prevents goals and also has the most chances to score them is by staying in control of the ball. Sounds simple, right? But remember, there are 11 folks on the opposing side trying to do the same thing! Keeping possession of the ball is tough but important, and leagues try to track how successful teams are at this with possession percentage.

Possession percentage can be calculated in a couple of ways. One of the most popular is by adding up the number of different times one team has the ball in its control, whether team members are dribbling, passing to each other, or shooting toward the goal. (The moment the team gets the ball to the moment the other team takes back control counts as one possession.) The sum of a team's possessions is then divided by the total number of possessions by both teams during the game and multiplied by 100 to get a percentage.

Possession percentage has been calculated since the early 2000s. It was inspired from the way that FC Barcelona played what it called "tiki-taka" soccer. Tiki-taka combines hundreds of short, quick passes, allowing a team to hold the ball for long periods of time.

In the 2018–19 Spanish league season, FC Barcelona led the way in possession percentage. It had a possession percentage above 61 percent. In a 2018 game, Manchester City in England set a Premier League record by recording an 83 percent possession rate, with a total of 942 passes!

SHANICE VAN DE SANDEN (LEFT) AND LIEKE MARTENS (RIGHT)

TONI KROOS

PACKING SCORE

Packing is an even newer stat, created in 2018 by some midfielders. These players felt that since they didn't score a lot of goals or assists, they were not getting counted as much in stats. With help from some video footage and soccer experts, the group created a stat they called "packing." Players earn points for moving the ball in certain ways, getting past opponents, or even for receiving passes in open areas. The more points in a game, the better their packing score.

AITANA BONMATÍ (LEFT) AND
DZSENIFER MAROZSÁN (RIGHT)

TRY *THIS!*

Track Your Stats

Time to play soccer … and stat keeper! Here are some soccer games that could end up with goals. Find a soccer goal, or set up your own with a pair of cones. Take turns with your friends playing each game and add up all the goals you score. You could even figure out your goal percentage: Divide the number of goals you make by the number of shots you take. Then multiply that number by 100. Who will be crowned as the top goal scorer in your group?

REMEMBER! Try these shots where there's plenty of open space.

Quick Shot

Work with a teammate to see how many goals you can each make in a minute. Player A is the first kicker. Player B retrieves the ball and returns it to Player A. Repeat until a minute is up. (Player B can use a stopwatch timer to keep track of time.) Player A shouldn't kick the ball too hard. That would mean Player B has to spend time chasing it down! Take turns and see how many goals you can each make.

Long Shot

Ready to go long? See who can kick a soccer ball into the goal from the longest distance. It can roll, fly, or bounce—as long as it goes in the goal. Who is the long-distance champ?

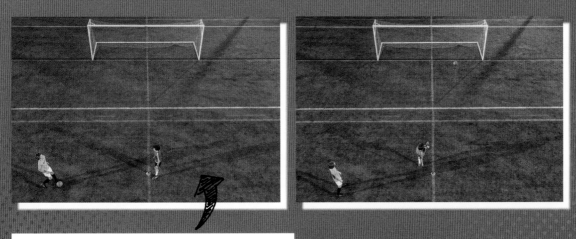

Little Help?

Combine assists and goals in this game. One player stands off to the side of the goal with the ball. The second player runs toward a spot about 10 yards (9.1 m) from the goal line. The first player makes a pass toward that spot. The second player runs up and hits the ball into the goal. You get one kick, no dribbling or trapping (stopping the ball with your feet). How many times can you score out of 10 tries? Then switch places so each player gets a chance to shoot.

STATSTARS

The longest goal ever recorded was 97.5 yards (89 m). It was struck by Stoke City goalie Asmir Begović in a 2013 Premier League game. His booming punt thumped down near the opposite goal and then bounced back up over the head of the other goalie.

CHAPTER SIX

TROPHY

TIME!

It's all about the hardware! That's a sports nickname for the trophies, medals, plaques, and more that teams and players win. Top-level players compete for two teams—their professional club and their national squad.

Pro soccer is played in national leagues, with all teams playing in a single country. Players, however, can come from any country to play in those leagues. Top pro clubs in national leagues also play in tournaments against other pro teams from their continent or from around the world.

For international play, national teams face off in tournaments that include a bunch of competing countries. The World Cup is one such event. National teams also play "friendlies," which are basically exhibition or warm-up matches.

In this chapter, see which pro clubs and national teams have taken home the most hardware!

STAT STORY

In each major soccer country, annual "Cup" competitions pit clubs from the same country (sometimes including amateur teams) against each other. In England, for instance, more than 730 club teams take part in the annual FA Cup (FA stands for Football Association). The fun part is that sometimes you get giants like Manchester United playing tiny clubs like Wrexham. In 1972, Hereford, a team from the fourth division, beat Newcastle in what one paper called "the biggest FA Cup upset" of all time. Watch the U.S. Open Cup games for the United States version of this type of competition.

THE MEN'S *WORLD CUP*

The biggest tournament in soccer—and some say the biggest sporting event on Earth—is the Men's World Cup. Run by the Fédération Internationale de Football Association (FIFA), the World Cup was started in 1930 and is played every four years. Just about every country in the world takes part in qualifying matches, which occur over the course of almost two years. In 2022, 32 teams will take part in the World Cup in Qatar. In 2026, well … we won't give it away. You have to wait until page 123 to find out!

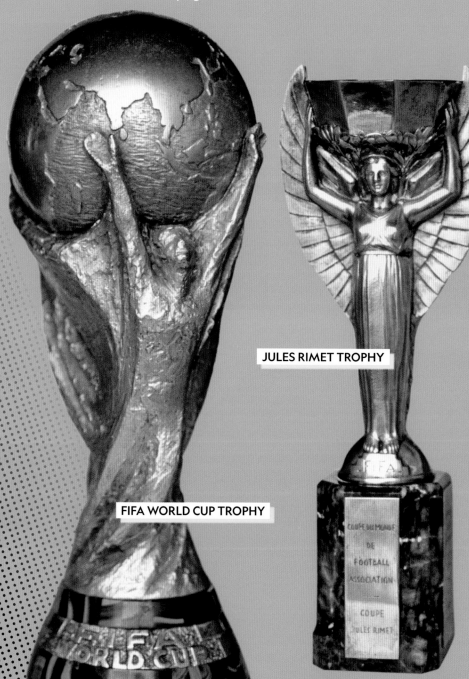

JULES RIMET TROPHY

FIFA WORLD CUP TROPHY

HISTORY BY THE NUMBERS

Brazil has dominated World Cup play. Their bright-yellow jerseys have ended up on the winners' podium five times. In 1970, they became the first team to ever win three World Cups. From 1930 to 1970, World Cup winners received the Jules Rimet Trophy (named after FIFA's third president). However, a rule said that if a team ever won it three times, they could keep the trophy and a new one would be created. So Brazil took its Jules Rimet home to Rio de Janeiro, and a new trophy was designed.

TITLE **WINNERS**

Here's how many times every victorious country has won the World Cup through 2018.

BRAZIL
5

**GERMANY/
WEST GERMANY***
4

ITALY
4

ARGENTINA
2

FRANCE
2

URUGUAY
2

ENGLAND
1

SPAIN
1

*After World War II, Germany was divided into two countries—East Germany and West Germany. Over the next 45 years, West Germany won three World Cup titles. In 1990, the two countries merged, becoming one Germany again. The reunified country then won a World Cup title in 2014.

97

THE WOMEN'S **WORLD CUP**

FIFA finally got around to starting a Women's World Cup (WWC) in 1991. That's right ... it took them 61 years to even things up. Well, it was worth the wait. The WWC has become a huge international event, attracting big crowds and huge TV ratings in many countries. The quality of play has improved each year. While the United States was the dominant country early on, many other nations have stepped up their game since then. Check out the top teams on the playing field.

WOMEN'S WORLD CUP WINNERS

YEAR	CHAMPION	RUNNER-UP
2019	United States	Netherlands
2015	United States	Japan
2011	Japan	United States
2007	Germany	Brazil
2003	Germany	Sweden
1999	United States	China
1995	Norway	Germany
1991	United States	Norway

TEAM GERMANY CELEBRATES THEIR 2003 WOMEN'S WORLD CUP WIN.

JAPAN'S FUTABA KIOKA AT THE 1995 WOMEN'S WORLD CUP

MEGAN RAPINOE REJOICES WITH TEAMMATES AFTER SCORING A GOAL FOR THE U.S. TEAM AT THE 2019 WOMEN'S WORLD CUP.

STATSTARS

Scoring goals at a regular soccer game is already awesome. When it happens at a Women's World Cup, it's a *really* big deal. At the 2019 WWC, Alex Morgan got the tournament off to a rousing start. The striker made five goals against Thailand! She also had three assists as the United States won 13–0. Then in the semifinal win over England, Morgan headed in her sixth 2019 WWC goal—on her birthday! That's a pretty cool birthday gift. Even better, those goals helped her earn the 2019 Silver Boot as the second-highest scorer.

STAT STORY

Many countries have started women's pro leagues in recent years. In the United States, several groups tried to start pro leagues but ran into financial problems. However, the National Women's Soccer League (NWSL) is the latest version (its first season was in 2013) and looks like it will be sticking around. It includes nine teams (and a tenth will be added in 2021), and each season wraps up with the NWSL Championship. Check out the champs who have led the league.

NWSL CHAMPIONS

Season	Champ
2019	North Carolina Courage
2018	North Carolina Courage
2017	Portland Thorns FC
2016	Western New York Flash
2015	FC Kansas City
2014	FC Kansas City
2013	Portland Thorns FC

THE OLYMPIC **GAMES**

Men's soccer has been part of the Summer Olympic Games since 1908. It was not played in 1932 when the Games were in Los Angeles—the World Cup had just started two years earlier and FIFA wanted that to be the biggest deal, not the Olympics. But the sport came back in 1936 because it was just becoming too popular to be limited to the World Cup. Women's soccer was added in 1996. Teams that qualify for the Games play in a mini-tournament leading to semifinals and the gold-medal final. A third-place game is played for the bronze.

TEAM NIGERIA CELEBRATES THEIR 1996 OLYMPIC GOLD MEDAL WIN.

NORWAY VS. BRAZIL AT THE 2008 BEIJING OLYMPICS

GOLDS FOR WOMEN'S SOCCER
The United States has dominated Olympic competition.

NATION	GOLDS*
United States	4
Germany	1
Norway	1

*As of 2019

GOLDS FOR MEN'S SOCCER
European teams got nearly all the golds until 1992. Since then, teams from South America, North America, and Africa have won the top prize. Nigeria became the first team from Africa to win in 1996. Check out the countries with the most golds for men's soccer.

NATION	GOLDS*
Great Britain	3
Hungary	3
Soviet Union	2
Argentina	2
Uruguay	2

*As of 2019

FERENC BENE (LEFT) AND JACK CHARLTON (RIGHT)

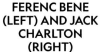

STATSTARS

ALL-TIME OLYMPIC GOAL-SCORING LEADERS

Men
Most overall: Sophus Nielsen, Denmark, and Antal Dunai, Hungary, 13
Most in one Olympics: Ferenc Bene, Hungary, 12 (1964)

Women
Most overall: Cristiane, Brazil, 14
Most in one Olympics: Christine Sinclair, Canada, 6 (2012)

AGNETE CARLSEN (LEFT) OF NORWAY
AND MIA HAMM (RIGHT) OF THE UNITED
STATES DURING A 1996 OLYMPIC MATCH

CONTINENTAL *CHAMPS!*

While the World Cup and Olympic soccer include all the nations of the world, continental soccer groups hold championships for the countries in their region. The soccer world is broken up into six such groups. Matches are played among the national teams in each group, and the best head to a tournament. One such event, the Copa América in South America, is actually older than the World Cup. Here's the scoop on these continental contests along with the countries that score the most victories at the events.

SOUTH AMERICA
COPA AMÉRICA
- Run by CONMEBOL (this is an abbreviation that stands for the South American Football Confederation)
- Sometimes includes Mexico and Central American nations
- First held: 1916

ALL-TIME CHAMPS:
URUGUAY

15 TITLES

EUROPE
UEFA EUROPEAN CHAMPIONSHIP
- Run by the Union of European Football Associations
- Formerly known as the European Nations Cup
- First held: 1960

ALL-TIME CHAMPS:
GERMANY AND SPAIN

3 TITLES EACH

AFRICA
AFRICA CUP OF NATIONS
- Run by the Confederation of African Football
- Held every two years
- First held: 1957

ALL-TIME CHAMPS:
EGYPT

7 TITLES

ASIA/MIDDLE EAST
AFC ASIAN CUP

- Run by the Asian Football Confederation
- Held every four years
- First held: 1956

ALL-TIME CHAMPS:
JAPAN **4** *TITLES*

OCEANIA
OFC NATIONS CUP

- Run by the Oceania Football Confederation
- Includes Australia, New Zealand, and other island nations in the South Pacific
- First held: 1996

ALL-TIME CHAMPS:
NEW ZEALAND **5** *TITLES*

NORTH AMERICA
CONCACAF GOLD CUP

- Run by the Confederation of North, Central America and Caribbean Association Football
- Was called CONCACAF Championship until 1991, when it became the Gold Cup
- First held: 1963

ALL-TIME CHAMPS:
MEXICO **8** *TITLES*

UEFA CHAMPIONS *LEAGUE*

Europe includes nearly all of the most famous pro soccer clubs in the world. Leagues in England, Germany, Spain, Italy, and France beam their games around the globe. You can find fans of the top teams in these leagues in just about every country. So it makes sense that the biggest club soccer tournament features the best teams in Europe. It is organized by the Union of European Football Associations (UEFA); to be soccer-cool, say "you-WAY-fah." Until 1992, it was called the European Champion Clubs' Cup. Now it's called the UEFA Champions League. Different name, same deal: Teams compete for the right to be called the "best club in Europe."

European teams that finish in the top four of their national leagues earn a spot in the Champions League. They are placed in groups and play in between their regular-season games. So making it to the Champions League means playing lots more games. Being strong and fit pays off almost as much as being super skilled. Fans around the world follow the Champions League match by match. The final playoff games toward the end draw huge TV audiences. Here are the greatest Champions League teams of all time.

LIVERPOOL PLAYERS CELEBRATE THEIR VICTORY IN THE UEFA CHAMPIONS LEAGUE IN 2019.

CLUB (COUNTRY)	CHAMPIONS LEAGUE TITLES
Real Madrid (Spain)	13
AC Milan (Italy)	7
Liverpool (England)	6
FC Barcelona (Spain)	5
Bayern Munich (Germany)	5

STAT STORY

In South America, the biggest pro club tournament is the Copa Libertadores. Each year, the top clubs from each of the continent's pro leagues face off. The event has included some of the greatest players ever, including Pelé, Diego Maradona, and Lionel Messi. It was first played in 1960. Argentine teams have won the most Copas. One of those, Independiente, won the most by a single club with 7.

EZEQUIEL BARCO

GEORGINIO WIJNALDUM WITH UEFA CHAMPIONS LEAGUE TROPHY IN 2019

DIGIT-YOU-KNOW?

Real Madrid got off to a hot start. They won the first five European Cups, from 1956 to 1960. No team since has repeated this streak of five in a row.

TOP LEAGUES

Just about every country in the world has a professional soccer league. There are hundreds of leagues around the world at a wide variety of skill levels. Some leagues, though, get more attention. The oldest and best leagues draw fans from around the world. Fans of Spain's La Liga cheer from Mexico City to Toronto to London. Supporters of England's Premier League gather from Chile to India to South Africa. Devotees of Germany's Bundesliga watch games from Egypt to China to Panama. Pro soccer is probably the most watched sport in the world. Here's a look at the best all-time teams in the most famous and popular leagues. They are listed with their country and first season of play. (All numbers are through the 2018 seasons.)

PREMIER LEAGUE
(England, 1992)
MANCHESTER UNITED 13 TITLES

LIGUE 1
(France, 1932)
AC SAINT-ÉTIENNE 10 TITLES

LA LIGA
(Spain, 1929)
REAL MADRID 33 TITLES
(It's worth noting that FC Barcelona has 26 titles. That means only two teams have earned more than HALF of all the Spanish league titles ever!)

BUNDESLIGA

(Germany, 1903)

BAYERN MUNICH **29** TITLES

MAJOR LEAGUE SOCCER

(United States, 1996)

LA GALAXY **5** TITLES

SERIE A

(Italy, 1898)

JUVENTUS **35** TITLES

EREDIVISIE

(Netherlands, 1891)

AFC AJAX **34** TITLES

DIGIT-YOU-KNOW?

The longest undefeated run by a club was achieved by Steaua Bucureşti, a club in Romania. Between 1986 and 1989, Steaua Bucureşti won 119 matches in a row! That's an all-time club record.

TRY *THIS!*

Hold a World Cup

Ask family members about the regions or countries where your family comes from originally, or just think of some countries you're interested in. Narrow it down to one country. Have your friends and neighbors do the same. (Just don't pick the same countries.) Look up the names of each one's pro league. Find out how many teams play in it. Have any of these countries won a World Cup? Now that you're well informed, form teams for each of the countries you researched. Come up with a schedule of matches. Have the winning teams from the first round play against each other. Keep holding rounds until one "country" is left standing. Whichever team beats the rest gets to hold the Neighborhood Cup!

Here's a head start on your World Cup research!

South Africa

16 Premier Division teams

0 World Cup wins

Brazil

20 Série A League teams

5 World Cup wins

England

20 Premier League teams

1 World Cup win

STAT STORY

Nearly all international stars play for the country they were born in. Some, however, qualify for more than one country. For example, if a player's mother was born in the United States and her father was born in Mexico, she could try out for either team. American star Christian Pulisic could have played for Croatia's team, for instance, because his grandfather was from there. The catch is this: Once you have played at least one major international game with a country, you can't switch!

CHAPTER SEVEN

11 CRAZY

NUMBERS

In every sport, there are numbers that, for big fans, need no explanation. In baseball, if you say "714," people know you're talking about Babe Ruth and his home runs. In basketball, mention "100 points" and a lot of folks will think of the time Wilt Chamberlain scored that many in one game.

Soccer has its own famous numbers. This chapter gives you the stories behind those digits. Start at the beginning, meet heroes new and old, see the sport change, and look to the future. All you need to know are the numbers!

DIGIT-YOU-KNOW?

Each season in England's Premier League, the three teams that finish at the bottom are "relegated." That means they are sent down one level on the ladder of pro soccer to a lower-level league. It also means that three teams get to move up. Earning one of these coveted spots translates to more money—a lot more money. Take Fulham FC, which won a 2018 playoff to earn promotion. Experts estimated that the move to the Premier League would give the team an increase in earnings of $214 million just in its first year. *Cha-ching!*

1863

The first two famous soccer numbers are years. Throughout the 1800s, various ball games were growing in popularity in England. In some, players kicked a ball. In others, they carried and tossed it. In still others, they did both! There were so many games, no one knew the rules and confusion reigned.

In 1863, representatives of multiple ball clubs sat down at a pub called the Freemasons Arms in London to talk about forming an official organization for the teams. Many of the clubs wanted the organization to be devoted to the kicking-only type of game. But there were also clubs that were fans of the kick-and-carry version. After meeting again, the group held a vote. Those who wanted an organization dedicated to the kicking-only game won. And the supporters of the kick-and-carry game withdrew from the group.

From then on, there would be two "football" games in England. One was rugby football, named for the Rugby School where it started. The other was "association football," or just plain "football." That, of course, was the beginning of organized soccer. Soccer fans still make regular visits to the pub to see where it all began!

STAT STORY

While 1863 was really the kickoff to organized soccer as we know it today, the sport of rugby has a different famous number. And there is a statue to prove it. In 1823, Rugby School student William Webb Ellis was playing a kicking-only ball game when he suddenly grabbed hold of the ball and ran with it. His classmates were astonished ... but then they followed him down the field! Some say this story is more of a myth than a reality. But over time, the idea of a kick-and-carry sport evolved into rugby. A statue of Ellis carrying a ball stands on the school's grounds to this day. It features a plaque with the year 1823 inscribed on its surface to honor rugby's storied past.

1930

The second famous year on this list came 67 years after the first. By the end of World War I, soccer had become more and more popular. It was played all over Europe and South America. Teams were starting in Asia and Africa, too. Each of the countries that had taken so strongly to the sport was sure they had the best players and the best national team. There was only one way to find out: have a tournament.

The Fédération Internationale de Football Association (FIFA) organized the first World Cup in 1930. It was played in Uruguay. Why this South American country? Uruguay had won two previous international tournaments, including the Olympic Games, where soccer had been included since 1908. (See page 100.) Thirteen nations, including the United States, sent teams to South America to play.

Maybe Uruguay got a boost from the home cooking, because they won the first World Cup. They beat Argentina 4–2 in the final game. As for the United States, the Americans won their first game 3–0 over Belgium. They also won their group and made it to the semifinals, where they lost to Argentina 6–1.

SOUVENIR FROM FIRST WORLD CUP

POSTCARD OF STADIUM USED
FOR FIRST WORLD CUP

HISTORY BY THE NUMBERS

Speaking of World Cup years, there are two that stand out for *not* being on the list. A World Cup was scheduled for 1942 but was not held because of World War II. The next scheduled Cup would have been in 1946, but the nations of the world were still reeling from the war, which had ended in 1945.

1–0

This is still the most famous score in United States soccer history even more than 70 years after it was tallied. In the years after World War II, soccer's popularity exploded around most of the world. In the United States, however, the game's popularity dipped dramatically. Baseball, American football, boxing, and even the new pro basketball leagues got more attention than soccer.

The sport was mostly played by immigrants from Europe, who often lived near one another in city neighborhoods. In St. Louis, Missouri, for instance, a large group of neighbors originally from Germany and Hungary all played in a city soccer league. When it was time to gather a national team for the 1950 World Cup, St. Louis was the place to look for players. Six athletes from this city were recruited to join the squad, which then traveled to Brazil. Because the American players were much less experienced

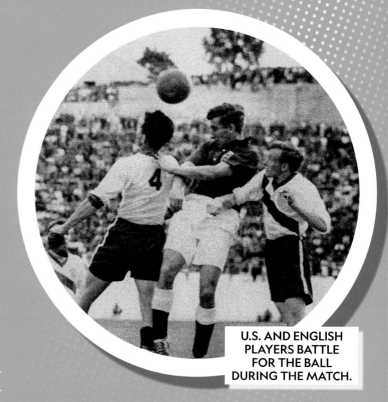

U.S. AND ENGLISH PLAYERS BATTLE FOR THE BALL DURING THE MATCH.

than players from other countries, few in the world expected much from them. The team's first match was against England, which had, after all, invented the game! The English were expected to swamp the Yankees.

But in one of the biggest upsets in soccer history, the United States beat England 1–0. The only goal was scored by Joe Gaetjens on an assist by Walter Bahr. Goalie Frank Borghi was also a star, making numerous amazing saves. It was the last game that the United States won at the Men's World Cup until 1994. Each time the World Cup rolls around, the story is told again of the American underdogs' surprising success!

THE UNITED STATES' 1950 WORLD CUP TEAM

HISTORY BY THE NUMBERS

Walter Bahr made a big play in the World Cup. His sons made big kicks in another sport. Matt and Chris Bahr watched their dad kick and copied him, but with a different ball. The Bahr brothers became successful soccer-style football kickers. Matt played 17 seasons in the National Football League (1979–1995), while Chris kicked in 14 NFL seasons (1976–1989).

IX

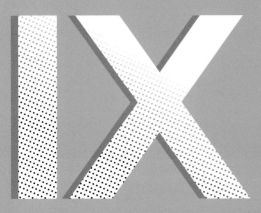

"**IX**" stands for "nine," if you're not up on your Roman numerals. It's an odd number, but it evened up the score for women in sports. Title IX was a small part of a long law passed in 1972 by the U.S. Congress about education in the United States. It basically said that from then on, schools had to provide equal opportunity in all areas for both men and women, including in sports.

Before then, women's high school and college sports were rare. While boys and men had lots of sports to choose from, girls and women had few. And the few they played were not funded well. Before the law was passed, one study showed that about 3 percent of college women played a sport. In recent years, that number is 40 percent.

Soccer was one of the sports that boomed for women after the law went into effect. Schools started soccer programs, and slowly more and more young girls got a chance to kick it on the field. In 1982, the first national women's college soccer championship was held. The growth of women's soccer in the United States helped create a huge pool of players for the national team. Other nations around the world were slow to catch up, and the U.S. team today is always among the world's best.

DIGIT-YOU-KNOW?

These teams have won the most NCAA (National Collegiate Athletic Association) Division 1 Women's Soccer Championships.

W	TEAM
21	University of North Carolina
3	Notre Dame
3	Stanford
2	Florida State
2	University of Southern California
2	University of Portland

ALEX MORGAN

1,281

PELÉ

We saw the number 1,281 earlier— it's the amount of career goals scored by Edson Arantes do Nascimento, or Pelé as he is known to everyone. But let's dig into it a bit more. Pelé is, to many experts, the greatest soccer player ever. He played in Brazilian pro leagues for 18 years, helping FC Santos win national and South American championships. For the Brazil national team, he helped win three World Cups; he was the first player to do so. He was so beloved in Brazil that he was declared a "national treasure."

In 1975, he came to the United States to play for the New York Cosmos of the North American Soccer League. The arrival of this all-time hero energized fans in the United States and helped the sport reach new heights of popularity. For a long time in the 1960s and 1970s, Pelé was considered one of the most famous people in the world, not just the sports world.

Since retiring, Pelé has been an ambassador of goodwill for the United Nations, a minister for sport for Brazil, and a promoter of the "beautiful game."

Some experts think the actual number of Pelé's career goals might be slightly lower than 1,281 due to miscalculations. However, the soccer world in general gives him credit for the total, and certainly no can argue with his genius on the field!

60 YARDS

Another player who some experts and fans call "the best ever" had his shining moment in the 1986 World Cup. Argentina's powerhouse forward Diego Maradona was leading his team in a key game against England. About 10 minutes after the second half began, he gathered a pass on his own half of the field about 60 yards (54.8 m) from the English goal. What happened next is soccer history.

Maradona weaved in and out amid a flailing English defense. He eluded five players as he dribbled at full speed. After making it into the penalty area, he cut the ball back (or kicked it in the opposite direction) to get around another defender and then just had goalie Peter Shilton to beat. Maradona faked him out too, and put the ball into the net. It was one of the most famous goals in World Cup history.

Maradona and Argentina went on to win the Cup that year. For his club teams in South America and Italy and Spain, Maradona helped win league and cup titles. To sum it up, when Maradona hit the field, he was magical.

DIEGO MARADONA

1994

The most important year in U.S. soccer history was 1994. This was when the United States hosted the World Cup for the first time. It was a make-or-break moment for the sport. If the event was a big hit and attracted big crowds, soccer might have a future in the country. If stadiums were empty, soccer probably wouldn't stick around.

What happened blew away all expectations. More than three million tickets sold quickly, the nine stadiums that were used rocked with noise, and hundreds of millions watched on TV around the world. The per-game average attendance of more than 68,000 fans set a World Cup record, as did the total attendance.

The U.S. men's team, encouraged by the home-country crowds, did better than expected. They beat Colombia 2–1 in the first round and made it to round 16 for the first time since 1930. Brazil ended up winning the Cup after a penalty shootout with Italy.

The World Cup drummed up $50 million in profits for the U.S. Soccer Federation, which used the money to develop more youth soccer programs. And most important, Major League Soccer (MLS) began in the United States two years later. Today, 24 MLS teams play in North America. And 1994 made it happen.

FIREWORKS GO OFF AT THE ROSE BOWL STADIUM IN CALIFORNIA, U.S.A., TO CELEBRATE THE FINAL MATCH OF THE 1994 WORLD CUP.

DIGIT-YOU-KNOW?

Here are the biggest crowds to watch soccer in the United States.   *Exhibition matches

YEAR	STADIUM	TEAMS	ATTENDANCE
2014	Michigan Stadium	Manchester United-Real Madrid*	109,318
2016	Michigan Stadium	Chelsea-Real Madrid*	105,826
1984	Rose Bowl	France-Brazil (Olympics)	101,799
2018	Michigan Stadium	Liverpool-Manchester United*	101,254
1984	Rose Bowl	Yugoslavia-Italy (Olympics)	100,374
1994	Rose Bowl	Brazil-Italy (World Cup)	94,194

1999

While the U.S. men's team has surprised the soccer world from time to time by making it to a World Cup, the women's team has long been among the world's best. In 1991, they won the first Women's World Cup, but the news barely made the sports pages. In 1999, however, soccer was much more in the public eye. The 1994 World Cup had created lots of fans, and MLS was helping spread interest, too. Plus, the 1999 Women's World Cup was played in the United States.

BRANDI CHASTAIN

GOALIE HONG GAO DIVES, ATTEMPTING TO STOP BRANDI CHASTAIN'S GAME-WINNING PK GOAL.

The Americans rolled through the early games, dominating the competition. They made it to the final against China. The game was played in front of 90,815 fans at the Rose Bowl in Pasadena, California. More than 40 million Americans watched a tense and dramatic game on TV. The overtime period ended with the score still tied. That led to a penalty-kick shootout. U.S. goalie Briana Scurry stopped a shot by China's Liu Ying. That opened the door for U.S. defender Brandi Chastain to bury her PK. When it crossed the goal line, the United States was the champion—and the spectators went wild. The celebration was on! Since then, the U.S. women's soccer players are among the most famous and popular female athletes in the country, regularly winning international events, including additional World Cups in 2015 and 2019.

91:00

The U.S men's team had a sudden-victory moment in the 2010 World Cup. You read earlier about extra time given by the referee to make up for when play stops. In a must-win game against Algeria in 2010, the United States used every second of that extra time.

The game was tied 0–0. If it ended that way, the United States was headed home from South Africa, the site of the Cup. Then in the 91st minute, goalie Tim Howard made a save and threw the ball to Landon Donovan. The midfielder sprinted toward the Algerian goal and then passed to Jozy Altidore, who pushed the ball along to Clint Dempsey, who smacked it toward the Algerian goal. The tall Texan's shot was blocked! Was it all over?

No! Donovan had never stopped running. He followed the play all the way to the end. As the ball bounced off the keeper's hands, Donovan pounced. He slammed the ball into the back of the net, earning the United States a dramatic win.

The United States had made it into the Cup's second round (made of 16 teams) for the first time since 1930. Though they lost the next game and were eliminated, the excitement of Donovan's moment still remains today. Donovan retired from the national team in 2014 as the all-time leading goal scorer in American history. None of his goals was more famous or more important than his South African shot.

CLINT DEMPSEY

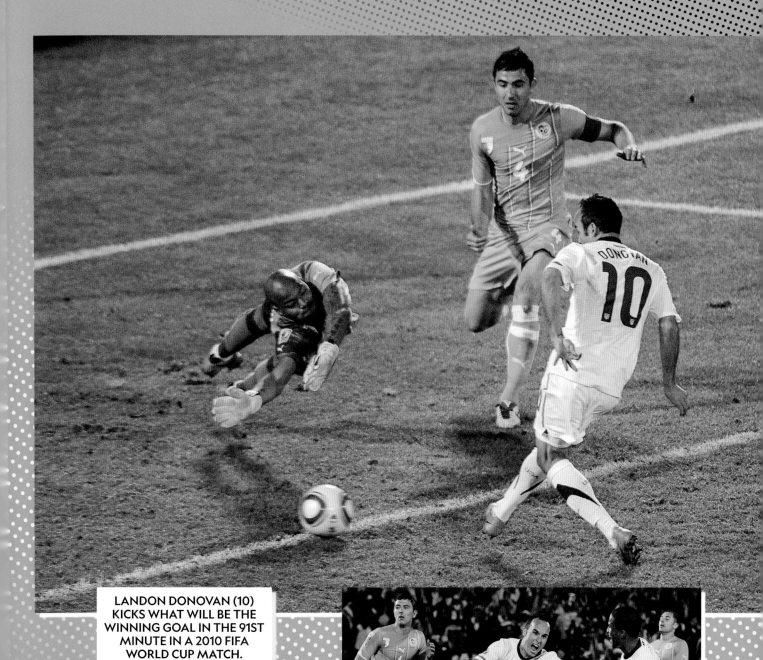

LANDON DONOVAN (10) KICKS WHAT WILL BE THE WINNING GOAL IN THE 91ST MINUTE IN A 2010 FIFA WORLD CUP MATCH.

STATSTARS

All-Time Goal Scorers: United States*

57	Landon Donovan (2000–2014)
57	Clint Dempsey (2004–2017)
42	Jozy Altidore (2007–2017)
34	Eric Wynalda (1990–2000)
30	Brian McBride (1993–2006)

*Through 2019

LANDON DONOVAN CELEBRATES SCORING THE WINNING GOAL.

DOS A CERO

If you're a fan of the Mexican national team, you might not want to read this section.

One of the fiercest rivalries in world soccer is between next-door neighbors Mexico and the United States. For a long time, it was a very one-sided rivalry. Mexico won or tied 26 straight games against the United States from 1934 up until 1980, when the U.S. team finally won a game. In 1991, the United States beat Mexico in the Gold Cup, a tournament of teams in the Americas and Caribbean. The score? 2–0 or, in Spanish, "dos a cero."

In 1997, Mexico flipped the script and won 2–0 in another tournament. It was the first time a Mexican team had won at a stadium in the United States since 1974. (All the other wins had been in Mexico.) Things got numerically crazy after that. From 1998 to 2009, the United States played Mexico three times in World Cup qualifying games in American stadiums. *All* those games ended 2–0 in favor of the United States.

THE UNITED STATES VS. MEXICO IN 2013

In the middle of those was a shocking win over Mexico during the 2002 World Cup. Guess what the score was? That victory ended Mexico's run at that event and put the United States into the final eight for the first time in its World Cup history.

Wait, there's more! In 2013, the United States won again by a score of—all together now!—"dos a cero!" The win clinched the U.S. team's spot in the 2014 World Cup.

In all, the two countries have played 66 times over the years. Of these, 13 games have ended exactly two to nothing, with either team on top. In recent years, so many of those have gone the Americans' way that "dos a cero" is not something you should say very loud if you visit Mexico City!

DIGIT-YOU-KNOW?

Here is how the men's United States team has done against its most played opponents.

OPPONENT	W	L	D*
Mexico	19	36	15
Costa Rica	17	16	6
Canada	15	9	12
Guatemala	16	5	6
Trinidad and Tobago	19	3	5

*D stands for "draw," the soccer word for a tie!

48

The final "crazy number" is one that hasn't officially happened yet. What does that mean? Well, since 1998 the World Cup has included the top 32 teams in the world. Before that, it was 24 teams from 1982 to 1994 and 16 teams from 1950 to 1978.

With the ongoing boom of soccer around the world and the piles of money that the World Cup makes for FIFA ($6.1 billion in 2018), the leaders of the sport decided to let the Cup grow again. Starting in 2026, 48 teams will make it to the World Cup.

In 2026, the United States, Canada, and Mexico will share hosting duties. Sixteen cities will be chosen to host games. Canada and Mexico will get 10 games each, with the rest in the United States, including from the quarterfinals onward.

One possibility is that there will be 16 groups of three teams and that the top two teams from each group will make the knockout round of 32. But there could be other ways to arrange it. Some smaller nations in Europe are thrilled because they might have a shot at their first Cup. African nations figure to gain the most teams, while participation from Asian countries will probably increase, too.

There are a lot of things to figure out before the games begin, but this number is a big one. It shows just how huge soccer is around the world and how much bigger it continues to get. Keep watching—maybe the 2046 World Cup will include 64 teams!

PERFORMERS REHEARSE FOR THE 1994 WORLD CUP OPENING CEREMONIES.

SOCCER STADIUM IN MEXICO CITY, MEXICO

GLOSSARY

area: number of square units that cover the surface of a closed figure

assist: a pass that leads directly to a goal

cap: an honorary acknowledgment given to a player for each national team game played in

circumference: the distance around a circle

clean sheet: slang for when a goalie doesn't allow any goals scored

defender: soccer position that plays nearest to the goal to prevent scoring

diameter: the distance across the middle of a circle

dribbling: giving the ball little continuous kicks while running

forward: soccer position that plays nearest the opponent's goal to score goals

foul: an illegal play

free kick: a kick awarded by the referee to the team that has been fouled

kit: British term for soccer gear

midfielder: soccer position that makes passes between defenders and forwards

penalty kick: a free kick awarded for a foul in the penalty box, taken against just the goalie from 12 yards (11 m)

pitch: the soccer field

retired number: a uniform or jersey number that a pro team sets aside to honor a great player; the number will never be issued again

spin: a rotation of the ball

trajectory: the path followed by a moving object

World Cup: the international championship of soccer, held every four years with separate events for men and women

ABBREVIATIONS

AYSO	American Youth Soccer Organization
FIFA	Fédération Internationale de Football Association
MLS	Major League Soccer
NWSL	National Women's Soccer League
PK	penalty kick
UEFA	Union of European Football Associations
VAR	video assistant referee
WC	World Cup
WWC	Women's World Cup

CREDITS

INDEX

Illustrations are indicated by **boldface.**

A

AFC Asian Cup 103
Africa Cup of Nations 102
Alves, Diego **67,** 87, **87**
American Youth Soccer Organization (AYSO) 17, 27
Assistant referees 20, 30, 31
Assists 88–89, **88–89**
Audi Player Index 53

B

Bahr, Walter 114
Beach soccer 11, **11,** 17
Beckenbauer, Franz 37, **37**
Beckham, David 37, **37,** 49, **49**
Begovic, Asmir 93
Bending the ball 48–49, **49,** 79
Bradley, Michael 37, **37**
Buffon, Gianluigi 36
Bundesliga 63, 84, 106, 107

C

Cafu 36
Cameras 56–58, **57, 58**
Carlos, Roberto 36, **36**
Carlsen, Agnete 101, **101**
Cech, Petr 87, **87**
Center circle **10,** 20
Chastain, Brandi 37, **37,** 73, 119, **119**
Clean sheets 36, 87
Clocks and timekeeping 18, **18,** 20
CONCACAF Gold Cup 103

Copa América 102
Corner kicks 21, **21,** 79, 80
Cricket (sport) 10, 55
Cruyff, Johan 39, **39**

D

Daei, Ali 81, **81**
Daems, Flip 72, **72**
Defender (position) 28, 34, 46, 47, 51, 53
Dempsey, Clint 120, **120,** 121
Di Stéfano, Alfredo 38
Dinamite, Roberto 85, **85**
Distance run (stat) 52, 54–55
Donovan, Landon 38, 120, **121**
Dribbling 46, **46,** 47, **60,** 60–61
Drogba, Didier 39, **39**

E

Ellis, William Webb 112, **112**

F

Fédération Internationale de Football Association (FIFA) 10, 89, 96, 100, 113, 123
Field markings **10,** 12
Fontaine, Just 82, **82**
Football, American 10, 32, 114
Formations, player 28–29, **28–29,** 32, 40–41, 50
Forward (position) 28, 35, 53
Fouls 12, 21, 30, 31, 59, 79
Fourth official 18, 31

Free kicks 21, 30, 49, **49,** 68, 69, 79, 80
Freemasons Arms (pub), London, England 112, **112**
Futsal (game) 11, **11,** 17

G

Gerrard, Steven 38, **38**
Giggs, Ryan 88
Goal box 12, **13**
Goal dimensions 14
Goal-line technology 56–57, **56–57,** 59
Goalkeeping
  geometry of 64–65, **64–65**
  how to practice 74, **74–75**
  protection of near post 66, **66,** 67
  stats 86–87
  stopping penalty kicks 23, 72–73, **73**
Golden Glove (award) 74, **74**
Greaves, Jimmy 84, **84**
Groenen, Jackie 50, **50**

H

Hamm, Mia 38, **38,** 80, 88, **88, 101**
Headers 35, **35,** 78, **78**
Hong Gao 119
Howard, Tim **71,** 86, **86,** 120

I

Ibrahimovic, Zlatan 81

J

Jabulani ball 44, **44,** 45
Jacobs, Francis 25, **25**
Jules Rimet Trophy 96, **96**

K

Kerr, Samantha 85, **85**
Kickoffs 21, 30
Kioka, Futaba 98, **98**
"Kits" (soccer gear) 33, **33**
Klose, Miroslav 82, **82**

L

Lampard, Frank 56, **56**
Laws 20–21
League standings, calculating 19
Lilly, Kristine 6, 80
Lloyd, Carli 80, 83

M

Major League Soccer (MLS) 10, 19, 35, 53, 118
Maldini, Paolo 36
Maradona, Diego 39, **39,** 104, 117, **117**
Marta **35,** 38, 47, **47,** 80, 83, **83**
Messi, Lionel 39, 46, **46,** 84, **84,** 89, 104
Midfielder (position) 28, 35, 53, 91
Monitors 52, **52,** 54
Moore, Bobby 37
Morgan, Alex **6, 7,** 39, **39,** 80, 83, 99, **115**
Mühren, Gerrie 39
Müller, Gerd 82, 84, **84**

N

National Women's Soccer League (NWSL) 35, 85, 86, 99
Neuer, Manuel 65, **65**
Neville, Gary 34, **34,** 36, **36**

O

OFC Nations Cup 103
Olympic Games 66, 100–101, **100–101,** 102, 113, 118

P

Packing score (stat) 91
Pelé 38, **38,** 81, 82, 104, 116, **116**
Penalty area 12–13, 20, 21, 59, 62, 65, 70
Penalty kicks
  assists 89
  goals from 12, 72, **72,** 79, 80, 87, 119, **119**
  law 21
  shootouts 19, 22–23, **22–23,** 119
  stopping 23, 72–73, **73,** 87
  VAR system 58, 59
Perisic, Ivan 54, **54**
Piola, Silvio 84, **84**
Players, number of 26
Positions 28, 32, 34
Possession percentage (stat) 90
Premier League 54, 63, 87, 88, 90, 93, 106, 111

R

Ramos, Sergio 37
Rapinoe, Megan 99, **99**
Red cards **20,** 30, 31, 59, **59**
Referees 20, **30,** 30–31, **31**
  instant-replay video 58–59
  mistakes by 56
  number of 20, 30, 56
  timekeeping by 18, 20
Retired numbers 36

Ronaldo, Cristiano 37, 81, **81,** 82
Rugby 55, 112
Rules 20–21

S

Scurry, Briana 73, **73,** 119
"Set piece" goals 80
Shots on goal (stat) 63
"Soccer" (word): origin 10
Soccer balls
  design history 16, 44
  size chart 17
  speeds and flight paths 16, 44, 45
Solo, Hope 36, **36, 70**
Stadiums
  biggest soccer crowds 118
  camera technology **56–57,** 57
  seating capacities 9
  World Cup postcard (1930) **113**
Suele, Niklas **34**
Sun Wen 80, 83

T

Taider, Saphir 53, **53**
Telstar pattern 44, **44**
"Tiki-taka" soccer 90
Triangle offense 50–51, **50–51**
Trophies **94,** 95, 96, **96,** 98, 105

U

UEFA Champions League 104–105
Ulreich, Sven 72, **72**
Uniforms
  jersey numbers 32, 34–39
  players' "kits" 33, **33**

rules 20
team jerseys sold to fans 33
Union of European Football Associations (UEFA) 102, 104–105

V

Video assistant referee (VAR) system **58,** 58–59

W

Walker, Natalie 18, **18**
Walls, defensive 48, 49, **49,** 68–69, **68–69**
Wambach, Abby 6, 80, **80,** 83
Wijnaldum, Georginio 105, **105**
Williams, Lydia 86, **86**
Women's World Cup 54, 73, **73,** 83, 98–99, 98–99, 119, **119**
Wondolowski, Chris 85, **85**
World Cup
  first (1930) 112, **112**
  hosted by United States (1994) 118, **118**
  referee mistakes 56
  scoring leaders 82–83
  specially made balls 44, **44**
  title winners 97, **97**
  trophies 96, **96**
  United States vs. England (1950) 114, **114**

Y

Yankey, Rachel 49, **49**
Yellow cards 30, 31, **31,** 59

MATH TEACHER REFERENCE

ALGEBRA: page 19

GEOMETRY
- **Angles:** pages 46, 47, 64, 68, and 77
- **Shapes:** pages 16, 44, 45, and 50

MEASUREMENT: pages 10, 12, 14, and 17

PERCENTAGES: pages 27, 72, 73, 86, 87, and 90

RATES: pages 52 and 53

STATISTICS
- **Averages:** page 63
- **Bar graphs:** pages 27 and 55

Since 1888, the National Geographic Society has funded more than 14,000 research, conservation, education, and storytelling projects around the world. National Geographic Partners distributes a portion of the funds it receives from your purchase to National Geographic Society to support programs including the conservation of animals and their habitats. To learn more, visit natgeo.com/info.

For more information, visit nationalgeographic.com, call 1-877-873-6846, or write to the following address:

National Geographic Partners, LLC
1145 17th Street N.W.
Washington, DC 20036-4688 U.S.A.

For librarians and teachers: nationalgeographic.com/books/librarians-and-educators/
More for kids from National Geographic: natgeokids.com

This is for all the youth soccer coaches out there who give so much of their time and energy and love to help young people learn to play and enjoy "the beautiful game."

—JB Jr.

For rights or permissions inquiries, please contact National Geographic Books Subsidiary Rights: bookrights@natgeo.com

Designed by Julide Dengel and Fan Works Design LLC

The publisher would like to thank the St. James Complex for providing a space to photograph the activities in this book. The publisher would also like to acknowledge everyone who worked to make this book come together: Andrea Silen, project manager; Angela Modany, editor; Kathryn Williams, editor; Julide Dengel, art director/designer; Sarah J. Mock, senior photo editor; Mark Thiessen and Becky Hale, photographers; Robin Palmer, fact-checker; and Anne LeongSon and Gus Tello, design production assistants.

Library of Congress Cataloging-in-Publication Data

Names: Buckley, James, Jr., author.
Title: It's a numbers game : soccer / by Jim Buckley.
Other titles: Soccer I National Geographic kids.
Description: Washington, DC : National Geographic Kids, 2020. I Series: It's a numbers game I Includes index. I Audience: Ages: 8-12 I Audience: Grades: 4-6
Identifiers: LCCN 2019036139 I ISBN 9781426339233 (Hardcover) I ISBN 9781426339240 (Library Binding)
Subjects: LCSH: Soccer--Mathematics--Juvenile literature. I Mathematics--Study and teaching (Elementary)--Juvenile literature.
Classification: LCC GV943.25 .B82 2020 I DDC 796.334--dc23
LC record available at https://lccn.loc.gov/2019036139

Printed in the United States of America
23/VP/3

EXPERT REVIEWERS

Gail Burrill, now in the Program in Mathematics Education at Michigan State University, was a secondary mathematics teacher for over 28 years. She received the Presidential Award for Excellence in Teaching Mathematics, is a T3 National Instructor and elected member of the International Statistical Institute, and served as president of the National Council of Teachers of Mathematics and as president of the International Association for Statistical Education.

David Sanford is the Academy Director at Major League Soccer's D.C. United. He has been on staff for over 10 years and has completed several coaching licenses domestically and internationally, most recently receiving his Elite Formation Coaching License via Major League Soccer in conjunction with the French Football Federation. Before working with D.C. United, David played collegiate soccer at James Madison University and coached at the college level while on staff at The Catholic University of America.